TEST PREP MATH BOOK
FOR CASAS MATH GOALS 2 LEVEL A

Helping Learners Approach Math with Confidence while Preparing them for CASAS Math GOALS 2 Level A—**Forms 921M and 922M**

By

TABLE OF CONTENT

PREFACE 5

INTRODUCTION 6

HOW TO APPROACH MATH...7

STUDY STRATEGIES 8

CHAPTER 1: NUMBER SENSE AND OPERATIONS 9

Lesson 1: Understanding Place Value..9
    Practice Exercises 11
    Answer Key: 12

Lesson 2: Computing Using the Four Operations...............................13
    Practice Exercises 14
    Answer Key: 16

CHAPTER 2: CONSUMER ECONOMICS 18

Lesson 1: Using Measurement and Money 18
    Practice Exercises 20
    Answer Key: 22

Lesson 2: Using Information to Identify and Purchase Goods and Services......................23
    Practice Exercises 25
    Answer Key: 27

CHAPTER 3: ALGEBRAIC THINKING..29

Lesson 1: Applying Properties of the Four Operations.......................29
    Practice Exercises 31
    Answer Key: 33

Lesson 2: Determine unknown numbers 34
    Practice Exercises 36
    Answer Key: 37

CHAPTER 4: GEOMETRY 39

Lesson 1: Comparing Shapes 39
    Practice Exercises 41
    Answer Key: 43

Lesson 2: Solving Perimeter and Area Problems................................44
    Practice Exercises 46
    Answer Key: 48

Lesson 3: Measuring with Non-Standard and Metric Units................49
    Practice Exercises 50

      Answer Key: 52

   Lesson 4: Solving Problems Using Time and Liquid Volumes 53
      Practice Exercises 54
      Answer Key: 56

CHAPTER 5: DATA ANALYSIS AND STATISTICS...**58**

   Lesson 1: Interpreting Simple Data Sets, Bar Graphs, and Line Graphs....................................58
      Practice Exercises 60
      Answer Key: 62

   Lesson 2: Solving one- and two-step problems using bar graphs 63
      Practice Exercises 64
      Answer Key: 66

CHAPTER 6: PURE MATHEMATICS..**68**

      Practice Exercises 68
      Answer Key: 69

PRACTICE TEST 1 ....**71**

      Answer Key: 78

PRACTICE TEST 2 ....**79**

      Answer Key: 85

MORE TEXTBOOKS BY CBL **87**

About CBL **89**

PREFACE

Dear Instructors,

This Test Prep math book is specifically designed to prepare adult learners for the CASAS Math GOALS 2 Level A Forms 921M and 922M. It fully aligns with the CASAS Competencies and meets the requirements of the College and Career Reading Standards (CCRS), the National Reporting System (NRS), and the Workforce Innovation and Opportunity Act (WIOA).

Adhering to the CASAS test blueprint, this textbook covers mathematical areas through six detailed chapters: *Number Sense and Operations; Consumer Economics; Algebraic Thinking; Geometry; Data Analysis and Statistics; and Pure Mathematics.*

The book's content is structured to improve the mathematical thinking skills of adult students. It provides 12 lessons across various competencies, such as Consumer Economics, Community Resources, Employment, and Pure Mathematics. Each chapter is thoughtfully crafted with multiple lessons to foster deep understanding and practical application of mathematical concepts.

Additionally, the book includes two practice tests that simulate the actual CASAS assessments, incorporating real-world math problems to give students a genuine taste of what they can expect. Complete with answer keys for all exercises and practice tests, this textbook is a robust tool for effective learning and assessment.

Using this resource in your teaching will equip you to effectively develop and improve the math strategies, functions, and concepts necessary for your adult learners' success. Indeed, this book is an invaluable asset for programs that aim to empower their students with the mathematical skills required for success in everyday contexts such as community involvement, family management, and professional environments. To order class sets, go to **cbledu.com**.

INTRODUCTION

Dear Math Students,

Welcome to your journey toward improving your math skills with this test-prep math textbook. It is designed specifically for adult learners like you. This book is structured to prepare you for the CASAS Math GOALS 2 Level A test. In the six chapters, you'll explore essential mathematical areas, including *Number Sense and Operations; Consumer Economics; Algebraic Thinking; Geometry; Data Analysis and Statistics; and Pure Mathematics.*

With 12 practical lessons, this textbook offers a clear path to improving your mathematical knowledge.

Practicing the exercises in this book is crucial. Each chapter includes multiple lessons that build on each other to help you understand and apply mathematical concepts in real-world situations. By engaging with these exercises, you'll develop a stronger foundation in each topic, making sure that you're well-prepared not just for the tests but also for the practical application of these skills in daily life.

We've also included two practice tests that mimic the actual CASAS level A test. These practice tests are designed to give you a realistic experience of what to expect on the actual test. By taking these practice tests, you can assess your progress, identify areas where you need further practice, and build your confidence.

This textbook is more than just a study guide—it's a tool that will equip you with the math strategies, functions, and concepts necessary to solve word problems confidently. Regular practice and study will transform your understanding of math, turning challenges into opportunities for growth and learning.

Remember, math skills are essential for success in various aspects of your life, including community involvement, managing family finances, and professional advancement. By committing to completing the exercises and fully engaging with the materials in this book, you'll be setting yourself up for success in your academic pursuits and beyond.

Let's get started on this path together!

HOW TO APPROACH MATH

Here are ten practical ways you can overcome math fear and anxiety and build confidence while using this math textbook:

1. **Start Small:** Begin with easier problems that you can solve to build your confidence before solving harder ones.

2. **Practice Regularly:** Consistent practice makes math feel more manageable. Try to work on math problems a few times a week.

3. **Use the Book's Resources:** Take advantage of the tools and explanations in your textbook. They are designed to help you understand and solve math problems.

4. **Take Breaks:** If you feel overwhelmed, take a short break. Come back to the problem with a clear mind.

5. **Ask for Help:** Don't hesitate to seek help when you need it. Ask a teacher or a classmate, or use online resources if you're stuck.

6. **Stay Positive:** Keep a positive attitude about math. Remind yourself that you can handle it and that it's okay to make mistakes as you learn.

7. **Set Small Goals:** Break your math studies into small, achievable goals. Celebrate when you reach these goals to motivate yourself.

8. **Understand, Don't Memorize:** Focus on understanding the math concepts rather than just memorizing formulas. This understanding will make you feel more confident in your ability to solve math problems.

9. **Visualize Success:** Picture yourself successfully solving problems and understanding concepts. This visualization can boost your confidence.

10. **Reflect on Progress:** Regularly look back at where you started and recognize the progress you've made. This can be a great confidence booster.

By following these strategies, you'll be better positioned to tackle math with less anxiety and more confidence.

STUDY STRATEGIES

Here are ten simple strategies to study and improve your math knowledge, skills, and understanding using this textbook. Each strategy is designed to be practical and straightforward.

Strategy	Description
1. Set a study schedule.	Allocate specific times each week for math study and practice to build a routine.
2. Create a study space.	Find a quiet, organized space dedicated to studying to stay focused.
3. Use the textbook.	Read explanations and solve problems in the textbook to understand concepts deeply.
4. Practice with examples.	Work through example problems to understand how to apply math rules before trying exercises on your own.
5. Summarize each lesson.	Write a brief summary of what you learned in each lesson to reinforce your understanding.
6. Solve practice tests.	Use practice tests in the textbook to prepare for the actual test and build confidence.
7. Discuss with peers.	Study in groups or discuss problems with classmates to get different perspectives and solutions.
8. Teach someone else.	Explain math concepts to someone else to improve your own understanding and retention.
9. Use online resources.	Supplement your textbook with online tutorials and exercises (e.g., YouTube videos) for additional practice.
10. Review regularly.	Regularly go back and review previous chapters to keep information fresh and build connections between topics and chapters.

Using these strategies can help you make the most of your math textbook and your study time to build up your mathematical abilities and confidence.

CHAPTER 1: NUMBER SENSE AND OPERATIONS

Lesson 1: Understanding Place Value

Place Value System

In the decimal number system, the value of a digit depends on its place, or position, in the number. Each place has a value of 10 times the place to its right. Numbers in standard form are separated into groups of three digits using commas.

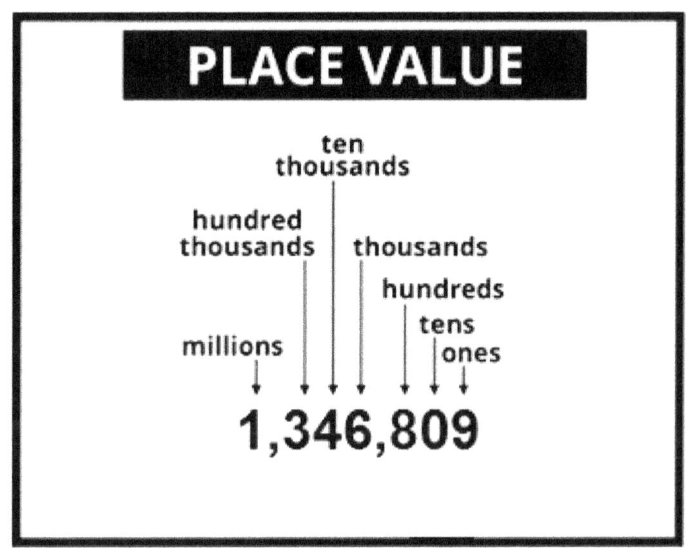

Numbers can be represented in several ways, but using the standard form is usually the easiest and shortest way.

Example 1:

What are some ways to show 1,951?

Solution:

Some ways to show 1,951 are:

Standard form: 1,951

Expanded form (as addition): 1,000 + 900 + 50 + 1

In words: One thousand nine hundred fifty-one

Example 2:

For the number 13,850, what does the 3 mean?

Solution:

Note that 3 is in the thousands place, which means it represents **3 thousand.**

To read and write numbers, we use **base-ten numerals.** Base-ten numerals tell us that each place in the number is ten times the value of the place to its right. To write a number in words, first break down the number in its expanded form, then combine the values into words.

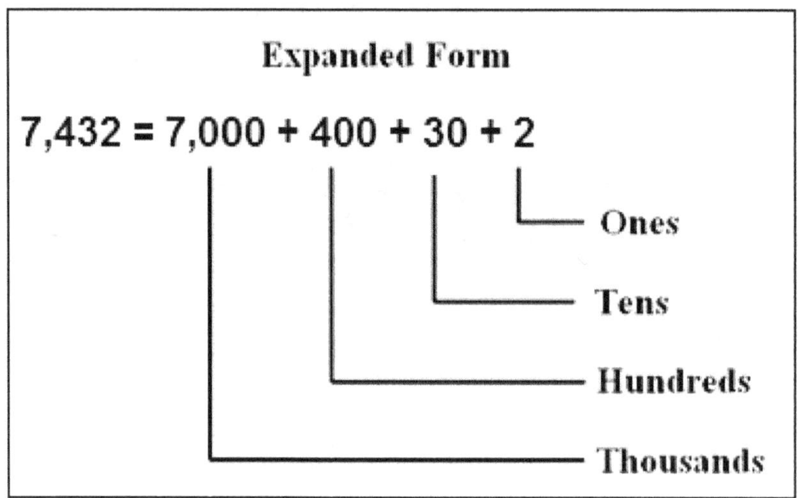

Example 3:

Write the number 729 in words.

Solution:

According to the place value, the first digit (**7**) is in the hundreds place. This means there are **7 hundreds** in the number 729.

The second digit (**2**) is in the tens place. This means there are **2 tens** in the number 729.

The last digit (**9**) is the ones place. This means there are **nine ones** in the number 729.

Thus, the number 729 in words is:

Seven hundred twenty-nine

1. Write 4,168 in expanded form.

   A. 41 + 60 + 8

   B. 4,000 + 100 + 60 + 8

   C. 4,000 + 160 + 60 + 8

   D. 4,000 + 100 + 68 + 8

2. What is the value of X?

$$6,823 = 6,000 + 800 + X + 3$$

   A. 2

   B. 200

   C. 20

   D. 22

3.

An elephant weighs 9,875 pounds. What is the correct way to write this number?

   A. Nine thousand eight seven hundred seventy-five

   B. Nine thousand seven hundred eighty-five

   C. Nine hundred eight thousand seventy-five

   D. Nine thousand eight hundred seventy-five

4.

A four-digit number has an 8 in the hundreds place, a 5 in the thousands place, a 3 in the tens place, and a 7 in the ones place. What is the number?

   A. 8,537

   B. 5,387

   C. 5,873

   D. 5,837

Tiffany wrote the following number in expanded form:
$$26,058 = A + 6,000 + B + 8$$

5.   What is the value of A?

A. 20,000   C. 200

B. 2,000   D. 2

6. What is the value of B?

A. 5   C. 500

B. 50   D. 58

7. What is the correct way to write the number in words?

A. Twenty-six five thousand fifty-eight

B. Twenty-six hundred fifty-eight

C. Twenty-six thousand fifty-eight

D. Twenty-six thousand eight hundred and eight.

8. What is another way to show 3,904?

A. 3,000 + 90 + 4   C. 3,000 + 900 + 4

B. 30,000 + 90 + 4   D. 390 + 40 + 4

9.   Which of the following numbers is seven hundred five?

A. 75   C. 7,505

B. 750   D. 705

10. Which number shows a 2 in the thousands place?

A. 257   C. 1,402

B. 1,283   D. 2,034

Answer Key:

1) B   6) B

2) C   7) C

3) D   8) C

4) C   9) D

5) A   10) D

Lesson 2: Computing Using the Four Operations

The four basic operations in Mathematics for all numbers are as follows:

> **ADDITION (+)**
>
> **SUBTRACTION (-)**
>
> **MULTIPLICATION (x)**
>
> **DIVISION (÷)**

Addition involves combining two or more numbers into a single term. It is denoted by the (**+**) sign. In addition, the order does not matter.

$$30 + 15 = 45$$

Subtraction gives the difference between two numbers. Subtraction is denoted by (-) sign. Subtraction is the inverse process of addition.

$$45 - 15 = 30$$

Multiplication represents the repeated addition of the same number. It is denoted by ($\times$). It combines two or more values to produce a single value.

$$6 \times 8 = 48$$

Division involves the sharing of an amount into equal-sized groups. It is denoted by ($\div$). Division is the inverse process of multiplication.

$$48 \div 8 = 6$$

We can solve problems involving the four math operations.

Example 1:

There were 28 gallons of water in a bathtub. Then, 12 gallons drained out. How much water is left in the bathtub?

Solution:

Notice that the problem requires the subtraction of whole numbers. Subtract the number of gallons that drained out from the total amount.

$$28 - 12 = 16$$

Then, **16 gallons** of water are left.

Example 2:

Wendy has 7 gift cards to the same store. Each gift card is $10. If she spends $50 of her gift card money today, how much will she have left?

Solution:

Step 1: First, find the total amount of gift card money by multiplying 7 by $10.

$$7 \times \$10 = \$70$$

Step 2: Then, Wendy has $70 in gift card money. To find out how much she will have left after spending $50, subtract $50 from $70.

$$\$70 - \$50 = \$20$$

Thus, Wendy will have **$20** left in gift card money.

Practice Exercises

1. During the summer, Nick was at the beach for seven days. Each day, he found eight shells. How many shells did he find this summer?

   A. 15

   B. 48

   C. 87

   D. 56

Look at the following weight scales:

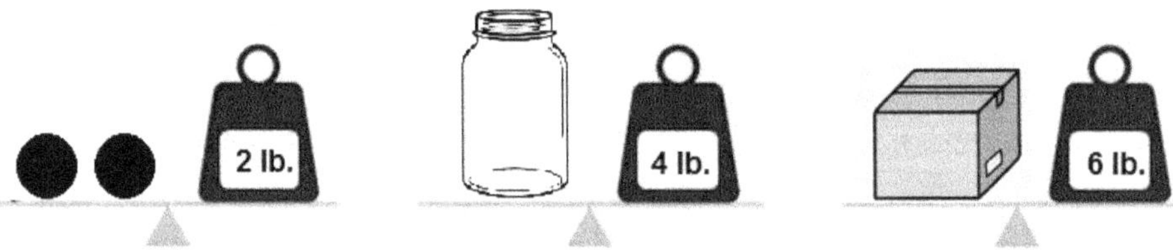

2. What is the weight of a ball?

   A. 2 lb.

   B. 1lb.

   C. 4 lb.

   D. 3 lb.

3. What is the weight of the box and five jars?

    A. 10 lb.   C. 26 lb.

    B. 15 lb.   D. 22 lb.

4. What is the weight of seven balls and six boxes?

    A. 43 lb.   C. 19 lb.

    B. 50 lb.   D. 45 lb.

5. What is the weight of a ball, two jars, and three boxes?

    A. 28 lb.   C. 25 lb.

    B. 32 lb.   D. 27 lb.

Look at the following math puzzle:

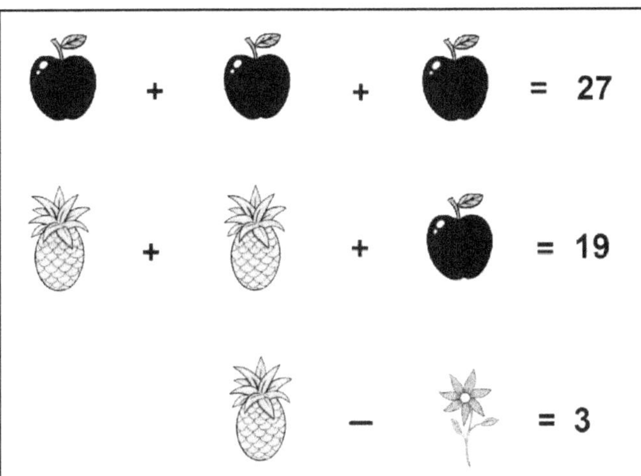

6. What is the value of an apple?

    A. 9   C. 11

    B. 7   D. 8

7. What is the value of a pineapple?

    A. 6   C. 5

    B. 4   D. 3

8. What is the value of the flower?

    A. 7   C. 4

    B. 2   D. 1

9. What is the value of five apples and four flowers?

   A. 45   C. 59

   B. 60   D. 53

10. Two items cost $51. If one cost $15, how much did the other item cost?

   A. $36   C. $32

   B. $38   D. $66

Answer Key:

1) D	6) A
2) B	7) C
3) C	8) B
4) A	9) D
5) D	10) A

REFLECTION ON LEARNING

Answer the following reflection questions and feel free to discuss your responses with your teacher or a classmate.

1- What math ideas and principles did you learn in this chapter?

2- What new math concepts did you learn?

3- What procedures or methods did you practice in this chapter?

4- What aspect of this chapter is still not 100% clear for you?

5- What else do you want your teacher to know?

CHAPTER 2:
CONSUMER ECONOMICS

Lesson 1: Using Measurement and Money

We can measure how long or tall things are, or the distance between things, such as cities. These are all examples of length measurements. Length is typically measured in *metric units* or *customary units*.

Centimeters and **meters** are examples of metric units.

Inches and **feet** are examples of customary units.

To measure lengths, we use tools such as rulers and yardsticks.

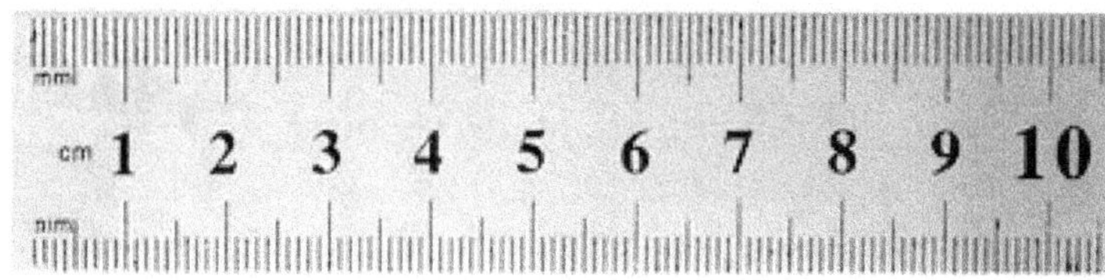

A **foot** is longer than an **inch**. There are 12 inches in 1 foot.

$$1 \text{ foot} = 12 \text{ inches}$$

When 3 feet are together, this is called a yard.

$$1 \text{ yard} = 3 \text{ feet}$$

When we put together 1,760 yards, we have a mile.

$$1 \text{ mile} = 1,760 \text{ yards}$$

Example 1:

Convert 25 yards to feet.

Solution:

We know that that 1 yard = 3 feet. To convert yards to feet, we **multiply** the number of yards by **3.**

$$25 \text{ yards x 3 feet} = \textbf{75 feet}$$

Example 2:

Convert 48 inches to feet.

Solution:

Identify the larger unit (feet) and the smaller unit (inches). Since we are converting from a smaller unit to a larger unit, we must **divide.**

Recall that 1 foot = 12 inches.

Now, let us find the number of feet in 48 inches:

$$48 \div 12 \text{ ft.} = \textbf{4 ft.}$$

The smallest unit of mass is **ounces (oz)**. A slice of pizza is about one ounce. If we have 16 ounces, it can also be called a pound (lb.). Typically, this is the unit that we use to measure the weight of people.

1 pound = 16 ounces

When we put together 2,000 pounds, we get a ton. In other words, we have:

1 pound = 16 ounces

1 ton = 2,000 pounds = 32,000 ounces

Example 3:

Convert 5 pounds to ounces.

Solution:

Identify the larger unit and the smaller unit. The larger unit is a pound and the smaller unit is an ounce. Since we are going from a larger unit to a smaller unit, we must **multiply**.

Multiply to find the number of ounces in 5 pounds:

5 x 16 ounces = **80 ounces**   *(Recall: 1 pound = 16 ounces)*

People use money every day, and being able to count it and work out how much change we should receive is an important life skill. The currency of the United States is the United States Dollar (USD). Its symbol is $. American bills, or paper currency, comes in seven denominations: $1, $2, $5, $10, $20, $50, and $100.

The most commonly used coins in U.S. money are quarters, dimes, nickels, and pennies.

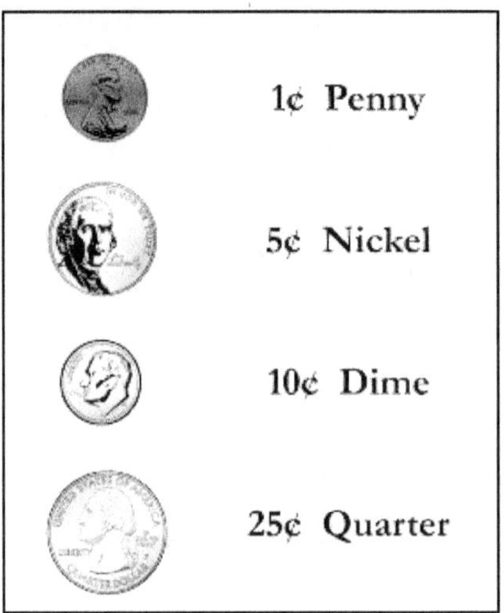

Some Dollar-Related Conversions:

1 dollar = 100 cents, so 1 cent is equal to 0.01 dollars.

1 nickel = 5 cents, so 1 nickel is equal to 0.05 dollars.

1 dime = 10 cents, so 1 dime is equal to 0.1 dollars.

1 quarter = 25 cents, so 1 quarter is equal to 0.25 dollars.

Example 4:

What is the total value of 6 quarters, 3 $10 bills, 10 pennies, and 20 nickels?

Solution:

Add the coins and bills separately, and then add the totals together.

6 quarters = 6 x $0.25 = $1.50

20 nickels = 20 x $0.05 = $1

10 pennies = 10 x $0.01 = $0.10

3 $10 bill = 3 x $10 = $30

The coins are worth $2.60. With the 3 $10 bills, that's $2.60 + $30 = **$32.60**

Practice Exercises

1.   A rock weighs 100 pounds. What is the rock's weight in ounces?

    A. 1,000 ounces   C. 1,600 ounces

    B. 3,200 ounces   D. 800 ounces

2. Which of the following is the smallest?

   A. 1 mile

   B. 1 yard

   C. 12 feet

   D. 12 inches

3. Dave has 10 dollar bills, 10 quarters, and 10 dimes. How much money does he have?

   A. $13.50

   B. $12.50

   C. $13.00

   D. $11.50

Look at the following bottles:

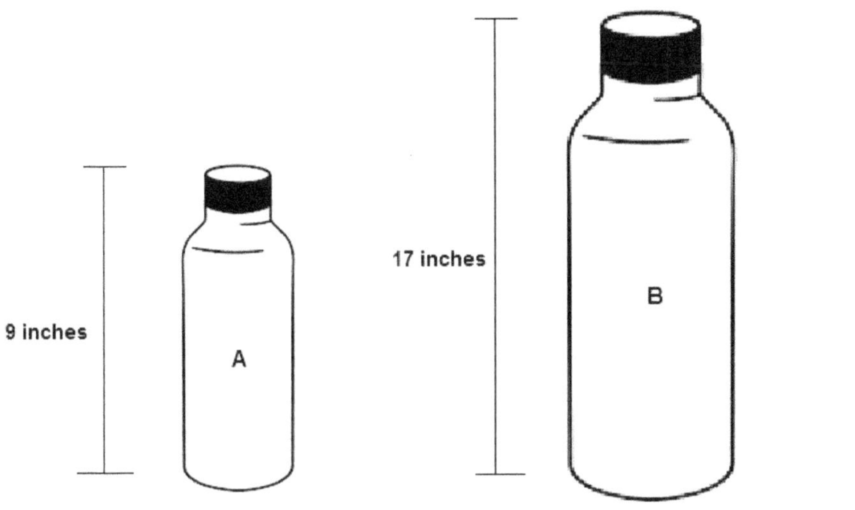

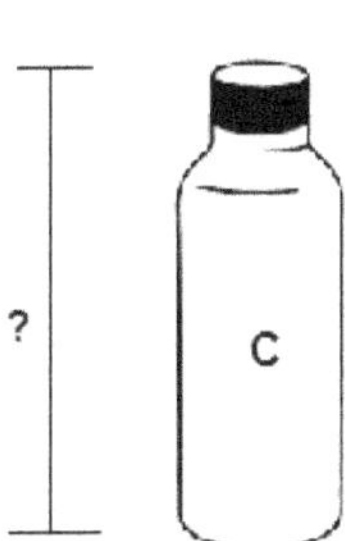

4. How much taller is Bottle B than Bottle A?

   A. 9 in.

   B. 8 in.

   C. 7 in.

   D. 26 in.

5. If Bottle A is three times taller than Bottle C, what is the height of Bottle C?

   A. 6 in.

   B. 5 in.

   C. 3 in.

   D. 12 in.

6. Which of the following is true?

   A. The height of Bottle B is less than one foot.

   B. The height of Bottle A is greater than one foot.

   C. The height of Bottle C is 6 inches.

   D. The height of Bottle B is greater than one foot.

7. Brianna claims there are X quarters in $25. What is X?

    A. 100   C. 150

    B. 50   D. 200

8. After buying some items for $8.50, James has $23.50. How much money did James have to begin with?

    A. $31.50   C. $15.00

    B. $32.00   D. $14.50

9. Danielle found 99 cents in a jar. She counted 2 quarters, 4 pennies, 2 dimes, and some nickels. How many nickels did she find?

    A. 25   C. 10

    B. 15   D. 5

10. Which of the following is true?

    A. 1 dollar = 20 nickels   C. 30 dimes = 5 nickels

    B. 5 quarters = 1 dollar   D. 10 pennies = 2 dimes

Answer Key:

1) C   6) D

2) D   7) A

3) A   8) B

4) B   9) D

5) C   10) A

Lesson 2: Using Information to Identify and Purchase Goods and Services

A good is a physical item that can be bought, touched, and used. A service is an action done for people who pay for it.

To obtain the best buy, we must compare the cost of two or more items and decide which one has the best value. This can be done by comparing the unit rates, which is the cost per item or per unit of weight/quantity.

To compare prices, divide the total cost by the weight or quantity of each item and then compare the **unit rates** of the items.

Example 1:

At Wonder Store, Steve could get 3 wireless earbuds for $54. At an online store, the price for 5 wireless earbuds is $80. Which is the best deal?

Solution:

Find the unit price for each place:

Wonder Store:

$$unit\ rate = \frac{\$54}{3} = \$18\ per\ earbud$$

Online Store:

$$unit\ rate = \frac{\$80}{5} = \$16\ per\ earbud$$

Then, the best deal is **5 wireless earbuds for $80** (lower unit rate)

Reading bills and receipts is a life skill because almost every household receives at least one type of bill or receipt each month. Understanding how to read bills and receipts can help us budget our money.

Example 2:

According to the following receipt:

a)   How many items were purchased?

b)   What is the total amount?

HerbalMedical

10 Ookmound Road
Chicago, IL 60628
Store#359   773-260-6457

```
1   @ 2 / 6.00                    $3.00
1   SODA DT 12PK                  $5.79
1   MCNX SEVR CLD CMBO 12Z       $25.79
1   MCNX SVR CLD LIQ 6Z          $16.49


SUBTOTAL:                        $51.07
TOTAL                            $51.07
MC (Swipe)
 PURCHASE                        $51.07
MC (Swipe)            3334
Auth#702468          Exp Date **/**
Lane #229            Cashier 874
7/17/2018  02:39 PM  Ref/Seq#96975
```

Solution:

Notice that **four items** were purchased. The total amount is **$51.07.**

Practice Exercises

Look at the following receipt:

```
         *  BURRITOS BUS  *

            Burritos & Tacos
        Voted Best Food Truck 2018
                SALE


     7/2/2018              12:31 PM

     Batch#:7538
     APPRCODE:7898          TO-GO
     Trace: 2
     Mastercard  -  insert
     1 Grande Burrito        $12.99
     3 Macho Fish Taco       $35.91
     1 Skinny Burrito         $3.69
     2 BTL Water              $7.96
     1 Beer                   $4.99



     Sub-Total:             $65.54
     Tax                        ?
     Total:                 $71.93
```

1. How many items were purchased?

    A. 5   C. 7

    B. 8   D. 9

2. What is the tax amount?

    A. $65.34   C. $8.43

    B. $12.99   D. $6.39

3. What is the total amount?

    A. $71.93   C. $71.50

    B. $65.54   D. $72.93

4. What is the cost of a Macho Fish Taco?

    A. $35.91   C. $11.97

    B. $12.99   D. $4.99

5. Which item is the cheapest?

    A. Grande Burrito   C. Water

    B. Beer   D. Skinny Burrito

A pizza shop has three different offers.

Offer 1	Offer 2	Offer 3
3 pizzas	8 pizzas	12 pizzas
$33	$80	$108

6. What is the unit price of Offer 1?

    A. $11 per pizza   C. $9 per pizza

    B. $10 per pizza   D. $12 per pizza

7. What is the unit price of Offer 3?

    A. $11.50 per pizza   C. $9 per pizza

    B. $10 per pizza   D. $8.50 per pizza

8. What is the best deal?

    A. Offer 1   C. Offer 2

    B. Offer 3

9. If Byron chooses Offer 3, what is the cost of six pizzas?

    A. $52   C. $54

    B. $60   D. $74

10. If Melanie chooses Offer 2, what is the cost of one pizza?

    A. $11   C. $15

    B. $12   D. $10

1) B	6) A
2) D	7) C
3) A	8) B
4) C	9) C
5) D	10) D

Answer the following reflection questions and feel free to discuss your responses with your teacher or a classmate.

1- What math ideas and principles did you learn in this chapter?

2- What new math concepts did you learn?

3- What procedures or methods did you practice in this chapter?

4- What aspect of this chapter is still not 100% clear for you?

5- What else do you want your teacher to know?

CHAPTER 3:
ALGEBRAIC THINKING

Lesson 1: Applying Properties of the Four Operations

Commutative Property

Commutative property tells us that in some mathematical operations, the order of the terms does not affect the result.

> *Commutative Property of Addition*
> $$A + B = B + A$$
> "Changing the order of addends does not change the sum."

> *Commutative Property of Multiplication*
> $$A \times B = B \times A$$
> "The order of the factors does not alter the product."

Notice that this property does not apply **to subtraction and division.**

$$8 - 3 = 3 - 8$$
$$4 \div 2 = 2 \div 4$$

✗ **Incorrect!**

Associative Property

When a math operation is very long, with many terms, we can group them in any way without changing the result.

> *Associative Property of Addition*
> $$A + B + C = (A + B) + C = A + (B + C)$$
> "We can group addends in any order, and the sum will remain the same"

Notice that this property does not apply **to subtraction and division.**

Distributive Property

According to the distributive property, multiplying the sum or difference of two or more terms by a number is the same as multiplying each term individually by the number and then adding or subtracting the results.

In other words, the distributive property shows how multiplication can be distributed over addition or subtraction.

We can use this property to division:

Example 1:

Find the sum:

$$18 + 26 + 12 + 14$$

Solution:

We can use the **associative property of addition** to group the addends in a different order.

$$(18 + 12) + (26 + 14)$$

$$30 + 40 = \mathbf{70}$$

Notice how grouping the numbers makes the sum easier to compute.

Example 2:

Find the product:

$$2 \times 4 \times 15 \times 20$$

Solution:

We can use the **commutative property of multiplication** to make operations easier to carry out.

$$(2 \times 15) \times (4 \times 20)$$

$$30 \times 80 = \mathbf{2{,}400}$$

Example 3:

Find the value of the following:

$$4 \, (15 - 9)$$

Solution:

We can use the distributive property of multiplication:

$$4 \, (15 - 9) = 4 \times 15 - 4 \times 9$$

$$4 \, (15 - 9) = 60 - 36 = 24$$

Practice Exercises

1. Which of the following is equivalent to $8 + 10 + 12$?

   A. $8 \, (10 + 12)$

   B. $8 \times 10 \times 12$

   C. $10 + 12 + 8$

   D. $8 \, (12 - 10)$

2. What is the value of C?

$$9 \times 8 = 8 \times \mathbf{C}$$

   A. 72

   B. 27

   C. 8

   D. 9

Look at the following drawing:

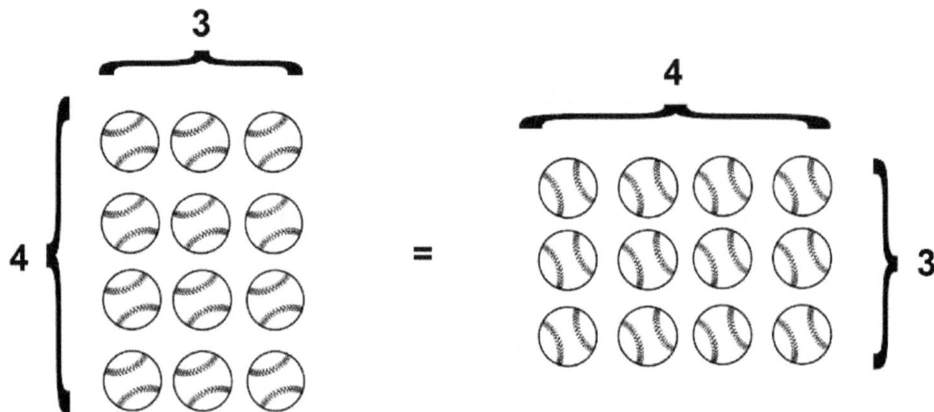

3. Which expression represents the drawing?

    A. 3 + 4 = 4 + 3   C. 4 (4 + 3) = 3(3 + 4)

    B. 3 x 4 = 4 x 3   D. (3 + 4) + (4 + 3)

4. Which property represents the drawing?

    A. Commutative Property of Addition

    B. Associative Property of Addition

    C. Commutative Property of Multiplication

    D. Distributive Property of Multiplication

5. What is the value of X?

$$4 + 8 + 12 = X + 12 + 4$$

    A. 8   C. 24

    B. 12   D. 4

6. The expression 5 (10 − 7) equals:

    A. 15 − 12   C. 50 + 30

    B. 50 − 35   D. 50 − 30

7. Which of the following is true?

    A. 30 + 9 = 6 (5 + 3)   C. (12 − 3) ÷ 3 = 4 − 3

    B. 5 + 10 + 15 = (15 + 5) + 10   D. 20 x 30 = 30 x (2 + 0)

8. Which expression is equivalent to 9 x 35?

A. 9 + 30 x 5

B. 9 (30 x 5)

C. 35 (9 + 1)

D. 9 (30 + 5)

9. What is the value of M?

$$4(8 + 10) = M + 40$$

A. 32

B. 12

C. 18

D. 48

10. What is the missing value?

$$A + B + C + D = (B + ?) + (A + C)$$

A. A

B. D

C. 2D

D. 2C

Answer Key:

1) C

2) D

3) B

4) C

5) A

6) B

7) B

8) D

9) A

10) B

Lesson 2: Determine unknown numbers

A **variable** is a symbol for a number we don't know yet. It is usually a letter like x or y, but we can use any letter. An **equation** is a mathematical statement indicating that two things are equal.

In an equation, the left side is always equal to the right side.

> **Equation**
>
> $$x + 4 = 10$$

To solve a simple one-variable equation, follow these steps:

1) Figure out what to remove. Look at the equation and figure out what is being added or subtracted from the variable. This is the number you need to remove.

2) Remove the number by using the opposite operation. To remove a number added to the variable, **subtract** that number from both sides of the equation. If a number is subtracted from the variable, **add** that number to both sides.

We can solve word problems using equations with a variable for the **unknown number** to represent the problem or simple contextual math situations.

Example 1:

Find the unknown number.

$$8 + ? = 22$$

Solution:

Step 1: Let x be the unknown number. We can set up an equation that represents the problem:

$$8 + x = 22$$

Step 2: Solve the equation. We need to remove 8 from the left side. To remove 8, do the opposite. In this case, subtract 8 from both sides of the equation.

$$8 - 8 + x = 22 - 8$$

$$x = 22 - 8$$

$$x = 14$$

Then, the unknown number is **14.** We can check it out.

$$8 + 14 = 22$$

Example 2:

Find the unknown number.

$$9 \times ? = 72$$

Solution:

Step 1: Let x be the unknown number. We can set up an equation that represents the problem.

$$9x = 72$$

<u>Note</u>: When a number is next to a letter (variable), this means they are being **multiplied.**

Step 2: Solve the equation. We need to remove 9 in the equation. To remove 9, do the opposite. In this case, divide both sides of the equation by 9.

$$\frac{9x}{9} = \frac{72}{9}$$

$$x = 8$$

Then, the unknown number is **8.**

Example 3:

Katie and Stephen buy candies. Together, they purchased 64 candies. Katie purchased 36 candies. How many candies did Stephen buy?

Solution:

Step 1: Let x be the number of Stephen's candies. We can set up an equation that represents the problem.

Number of Stephen's candies + Number of Katie's candies = 64

$$x + 36 = 64$$

Step 2: Solve the equation. We want to remove 36 from the equation. To remove 36, do the opposite. In this case, subtract 36 from both sides of the equation.

$$x + 36 - 36 = 64 - 36$$

$$x = 64 - 36$$

$$x = 28$$

Step 3: Then, Stephen purchased **28 candies.**

Practice Exercises

1. Find the unknown number.

$$? - 13 = 15$$

A. 2 C. 28

B. 18 D. 30

2. What is the unknown number?

$$50 + ? = 75$$

A. 125 C. 35

B. 25 D. 50

Mike wrote the following equations:

$$A + 17 = 44$$
$$3B = 30$$

3. What is A?

A. 27 C. 25

B. 17 D. 24

4. What is B?

A. 27 C. 9

B. 15 D. 10

5. What is A + B?

A. 17 C. 41

B. 34 D. 37

6. Twice a number is equal to 52. What is the number?

A. 31 C. 26

B. 28 D. 21

7. What is the unknown number?

$$? \div 2 = 48$$

A. 24

B. 96

C. 84

D. 46

8. What is N?

$$N \times 79 = 79$$

A. 0

B. 2

C. 1

D. 79

9. A number divided by 7 is equal to 7. What is the number?

A. 1

B. 14

C. 21

D. 49

10. $100 is shared between Mary and Luke. Mary's share is $43. What is the amount of Byron's share?

A. $57

B. $143

C. $47

D. $67

Answer Key:

1) C

2) B

3) A

4) D

5) D

6) C

7) B

8) C

9) D

10) A

REFLECTION ON LEARNING

Answer the following reflection questions and feel free to discuss your responses with your teacher or a classmate.

1- What math ideas and principles did you learn in this chapter?

2- What new math concepts did you learn?

3- What procedures or methods did you practice in this chapter?

4- What aspect of this chapter is still not 100% clear for you?

5- What else do you want your teacher to know?

CHAPTER 4:
GEOMETRY

Lesson 1: Comparing Shapes

In geometry, shapes can be classified into two categories: two-dimensional (2-D) and three-dimensional (3-D).

A **two-dimensional shape** is a flat plane figure or a shape that has two dimensions: length and width. Two-dimensional or 2-D shapes lie on a flat surface and have no thickness.

Two-dimensional shapes

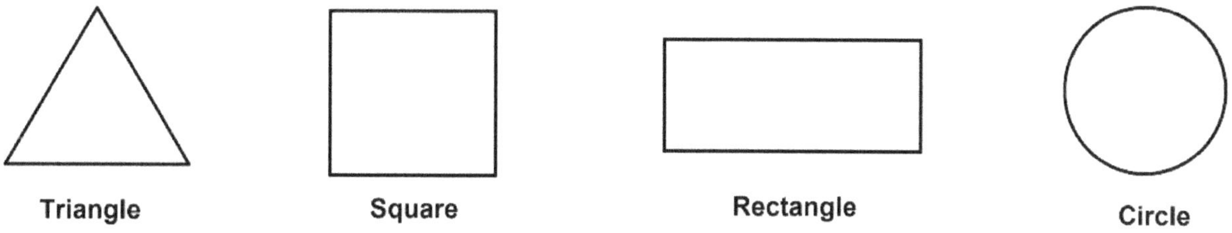

A **three-dimensional shape** is a solid figure or shape that has three dimensions: length, width and height. They have thickness or depth.

The key attributes of a 3-D shape are:

- **Faces**: The flat surfaces of the shape

- **Edges**: The lines where two faces meet

- **Corners (or vertices)**: The points where edges meet

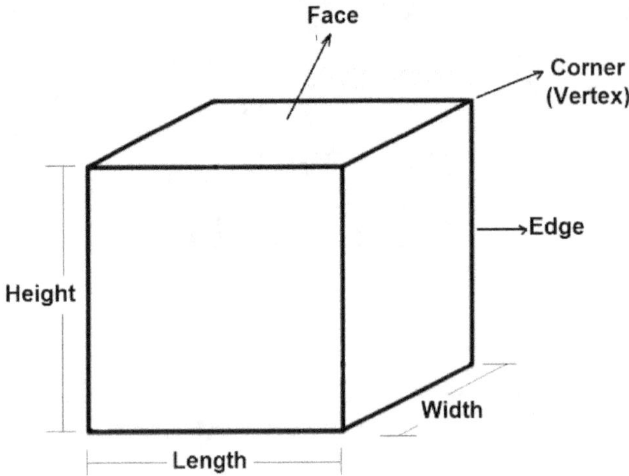

Three-Dimensional Shapes

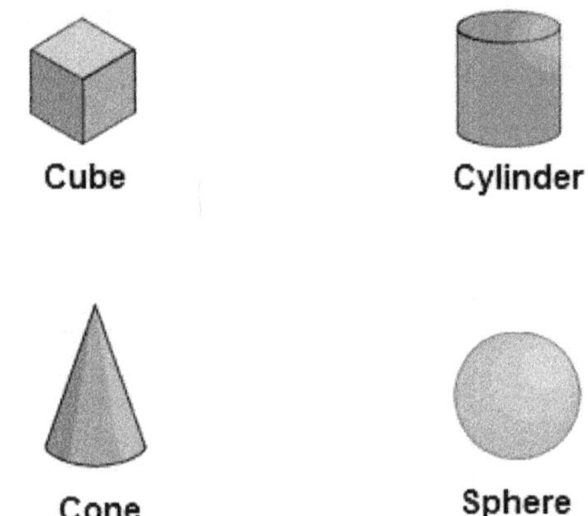

We can analyze and compare two and three-dimensional shapes in different sizes and orientations using informal language to describe their similarities, differences, and other features.

Example 1:

What is the difference between the following two shapes?

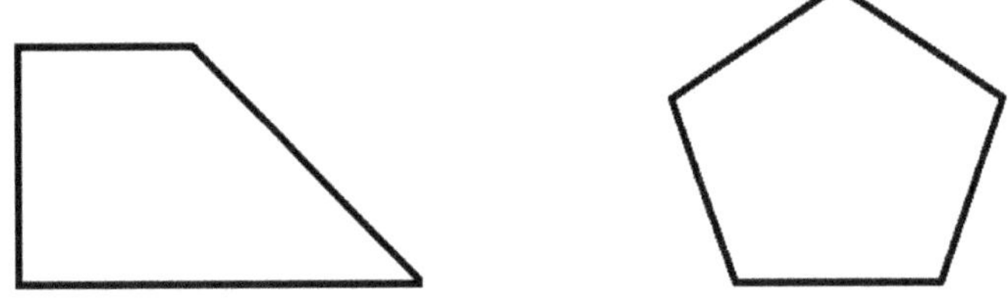

Solution:

Notice that both of these shapes are two-dimensional (trapezium and pentagon) because they are flat. However, there are differences in the number of sides.

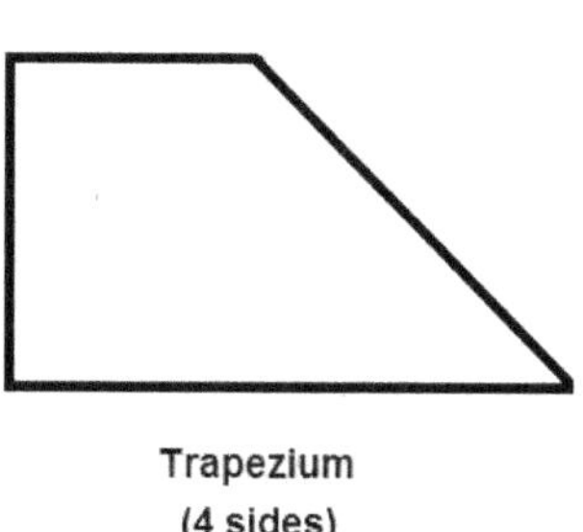

Trapezium
(4 sides)

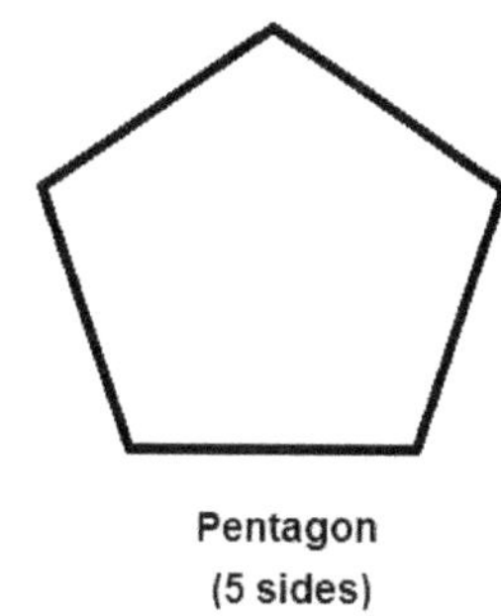

Pentagon
(5 sides)

Then, the difference between them is **the number of sides they each have.**

Example 2:

What is similar about the following two shapes?

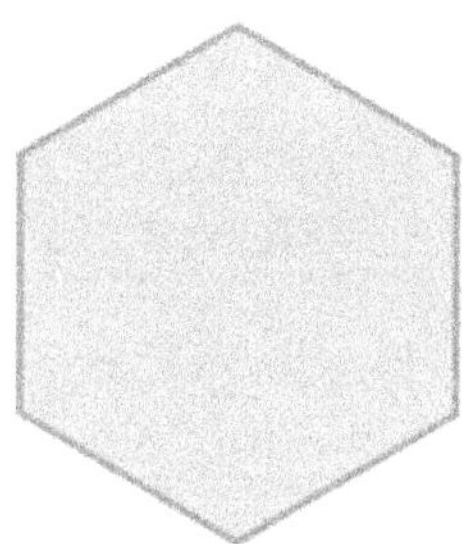

Solution:

Note that both shapes are two-dimensional because they are flat. Also, both shapes have **six sides and six corners.**

Practice Exercises

1. What is the difference between the following two shapes?

A. The number of corners

B. The number of sides

C. The number of faces

D. Their sizes

2. Which shape has more corners?

    A. Rectangle   C. Triangle

    B. Circle   D. Pentagon

Look at the following shapes

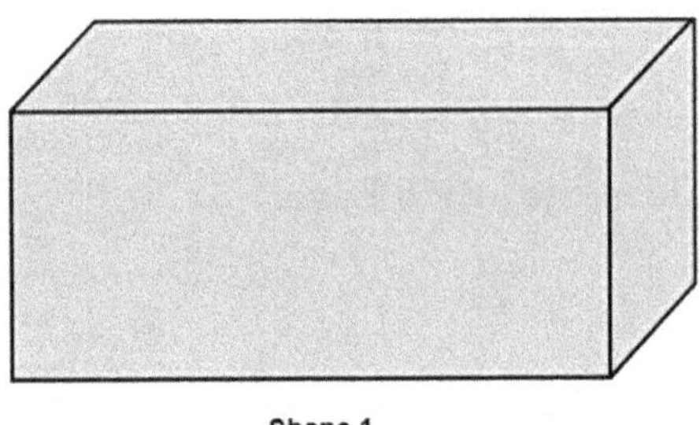

Shape 1

Shape 2

3. Which of the following is true?

    A. Shape 1 has three faces.   C. Shape 1 is a three-dimensional figure.

    B. Shape 2 is a square.   D. Shape 1 and Shape 2 are the same size.

4. What is the difference between Shape 1 and Shape 2?

    A. Their sizes

    B. The shape of the faces

    C. Shape 1 is three-dimensional, and Shape 2 is two-dimensional.

    D. None of the above

Look at the following objects:

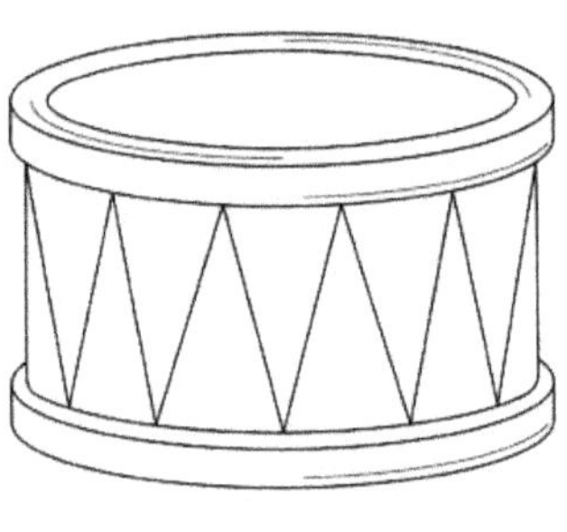

Object A

Object B

5. Which of the following is true?

    A. Object A has two flat faces.   C. Object B has three corners.

    B. Object B is a two-dimensional figure.   D. Object A has four faces.

6. What three-dimensional shape matches with Object A?

   A. Cube

   B. Cylinder

   C. Circle

   D. Sphere

7. What three-dimensional shape matches with Object B?

   A. Triangle

   B. Trapezium

   C. Cone

   D. Cube

8. How many faces does a cube have?

   A. 8

   B. 4

   C. 6

   D. 5

9. How are these shapes the same?

   A. Both shapes have three corners.

   B. Both shapes have two sides.

   C. Both shapes are the same size.

   D. Both shapes have a curved part.

10. Molly drew a pentagon and a rectangle. How many sides did she draw?

   A. 5

   B. 9

   C. 7

   D. 8

Answer Key:

1) D	6) B
2) D	7) C
3) C	8) C
4) C	9) D
5) A	10) B

Lesson 2: Solving Perimeter and Area Problems

Perimeter is the distance around a two-dimensional shape. **The area** is the amount of two-dimensional space inside a closed two-dimensional figure. A square with a side length of 1 unit, called a **unit square**, is said to have "one square unit" of area, and can be used to measure area. A **square inch** is a unit of area equal to the area of a square with sides of one inch.

The Perimeter and Area of Common Two-Dimensional Shapes

		Perimeter	Area
Rectangle	Length (l), Width (w)	$P = 2(l + w)$	$A = l \times w$
Square	Length (x), Width (x)	$P = 4x$	$A = x^2$
Parallelogram	a, h, b	$P = 2(a + b)$	$A = a \times h$
Trapezoid	a, c, h, d, b	$P = a + b + c + d$	$A = \dfrac{(a + b) \times h}{2}$
Triangle	c, h, a, b	$P = a + b + c$	$A = \dfrac{b \times h}{2}$
Circle	r	$P = Circumference = 2\pi r \text{ or } \pi D$	$A = \pi \times r^2$

Example 1:

Find the area of a triangle with a base of 6 feet and a height of 5 feet.

Solution:

Apply the formula of the area of a triangle.

$$Area = \frac{b \times h}{2}$$

Given:

- Base (b) = 6 feet
- Height (h) = 5 feet

Substitute these values into the formula:

$$Area = \frac{6\,ft \times 5\,ft}{2} = \frac{30\,ft^2}{2} = 15\,ft^2$$

Then, the area of the triangle is **15 square feet.**

Example 2:

Find the perimeter of the following rectangle:

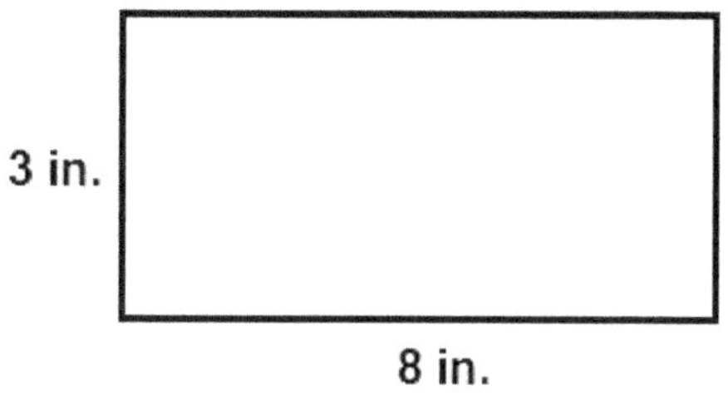

Solution:

Given:

- Length = 8 feet
- Width = 3 feet

Apply the formula of the perimeter of a rectangle:

$$P = 2 \cdot (l + w)$$

$$P = 2 \cdot (8\text{ in.} + 3\text{ in.}) = 2 \cdot (11\text{ in.}) = \mathbf{22\text{ in.}}$$

Example 3:

Find the area of a circle with a diameter of 10 inches.

Solution:

Apply the formula of the area of a circle:

$$A = \pi r^2$$

We know that the radius of a circle is equal to half the length of the diameter. Then, the radius of the circle is 5 inches.

$$A = \pi r^2$$

$$A = 3.14 \times (5\ in)^2$$

$$A = 3.14 \times (25\ in^2) = 78.5\ in^2$$

Thus, the area of the circle is **78.5 square inches.**

Practice Exercises

> **The side length of a square ground is 9 yards.**

1. What is the perimeter of the ground?

   A. 13 yards

   B. 36 yards

   C. 72 yards

   D. 18 yards

2. What is the area of the ground?

   A. 36 square yards

   B. 13 square yards

   C. 90 square yards

   D. 81 square yards

3. If Darrell ran three rounds of the square ground, what is the total distance he ran?

   A. 108 yards

   B. 27 yards

   C. 243 yards

   D. 100 yards

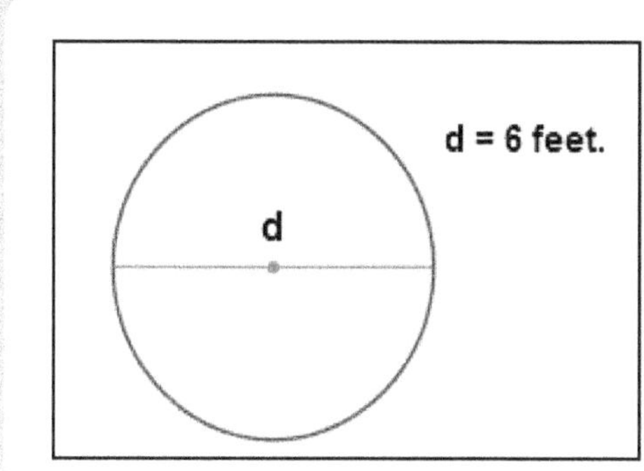

The diameter of a circle is 6 feet.

4. What is the radius of the circle?

   A. 12 ft.   C. 4 ft.

   B. 3 ft.   D. 5 ft.

5. What is the circumference of the circle? (Use $\pi = 3.14$)

   A. 9.42 ft.   C. 18.84 ft.

   B. 37.68 ft.   D. 21.15 ft.

6. What is the area of the circle? (Use $\pi = 3.14$)

   A. 18.84 ft^2 C. 9.42 ft^2

   B. 37.68 ft^2 D. 28.26 ft^2

7. What is the area of the following shape?

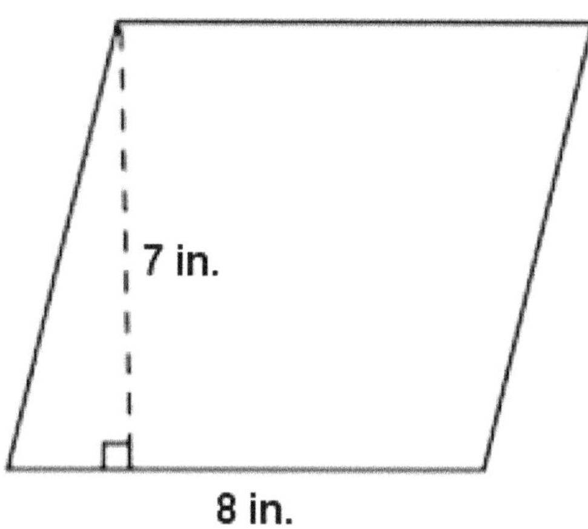

   A. 15 in^2 C. 45 in^2

   B. 30 in^2 D. 56 in^2

8. The length of the base of a triangle is twice its height. If the height of the triangle is 10 inches, what is the area of the triangle?

A. 200 in^2

B. 100 in^2

C. 50 in^2

D. 30 in^2

9. If the perimeter of a square is 8 feet, what is the area of the square?

A. 4 ft^2

B. 16 ft^2

C. 64 ft^2

D. 32 ft^2

10. The lengths of the sides of a triangle are 3 inches, 4 inches and x inches. The perimeter of the triangle is 12 inches. What is x?

A. 7

B. 9

C. 5

D. 10

Answer Key:

1) B	6) D
2) D	7) D
3) A	8) B
4) B	9) A
5) C	10) C

Lesson 3: Measuring with Non-Standard and Metric Units

Metric Units

Small metric units of length are called **millimeters.** The symbol for millimeters is **mm.** When we have something that is 10 millimeters long, it is said to be 1 **centimeter**. The symbol for centimeters is **cm.**

1 centimeter = 10 millimeters

1 cm = 10 mm

A **meter** is longer than a **centimeter.** There are 100 centimeters in 1 meter.

1 meter = 100 centimeters

Therefore:

1 meter = 100 centimeters = 1,000 millimeters

1 m = 100 cm = 1,000 mm

When we need to measure greater distances, such as how far we are going to drive or fly or the distance between cities, we measure that distance using **kilometers.**

1 km = 1,000 m

When we buy groceries, they are measured in weight units such as grams and kilograms. A **gram** is a metric unit of mass (or weight). It is abbreviated as **g**. A **kilogram** is a measure of mass (or weight). It is abbreviated as **kg**.

1 kilogram = 1,000 grams

1 kg = 1,000 g

Non-Standard Units

A non-standard unit of measure is a specified amount that is used to estimate the length, volume, or mass of an object. Non-standard units are everyday items or objects that are not part of the formal measurement systems.

Examples of Non-Standard Units of Measure:

Length – paper clips, pencils, hand span, cubit or foot span

Weight –apples, books, boxes or toy blocks

Volume –cups, spoons, handfuls or barrels.

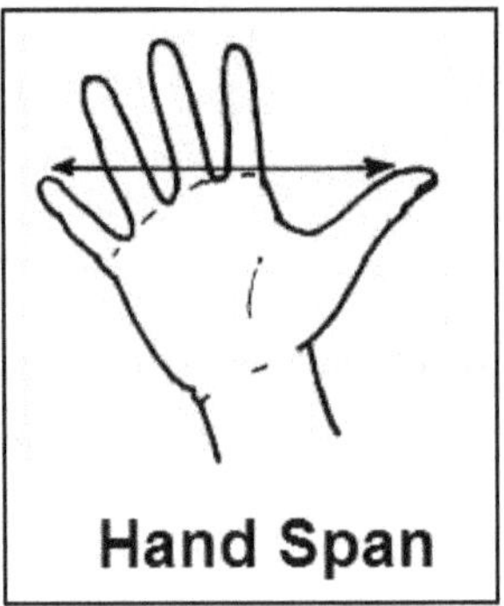

Example 1:

Convert 7 meters to centimeters.

Solution:

Identify the larger unit and the smaller unit. The larger unit is the meter, and the smaller unit is a centimeter. Since we are going from a larger unit to a smaller unit, we must **multiply.**

Multiply to find the number of centimeters in 7 meters:

7 x 100 cm = **700 cm**   (recall: 1 m = 100 cm)

Practice Exercises

Look at the following weight scale

1. Which of the following is true?

    A. An apple can be considered a metric unit of weight.

    B. the five apples are heavier than the soccer ball.

    C. The height of the soccer ball is equal to the height of an apple.

    D. The five apples weigh the same as the soccer ball.

2. Suppose that the weight of the soccer ball is 400 grams. What is the weight of the soccer ball in kilograms?

   A. 4 kg.

   B. 0.4 kg.

   C. 40 kg.

   D. 400 kg.

3. If the weight of the soccer ball is 400 grams, what is the weight of an apple in grams?

   A. 400 g.

   B. 90 g.

   C. 80 g.

   D. 40 g.

4. Suppose that the weight of an apple is 100 grams. What is the weight of the soccer ball?

   A. 500 g.

   B. 400 g.

   C. 5 kg.

   D. 4 kg.

Tony wants to measure the height of a house using a truck as shown below:

5. Which of the following is true?

   A. The height of the house is about three times the height of the truck.

   B. The height of the house is about two times the height of the truck.

   C. The height of the house is about four times the height of the truck

   D. The height of the truck is a metric unit of length.

6. If the height of the truck is 3 meters, about how tall is the house?

   A. 5 m.

   B. 4 m.

   C. 8 m.

   D. 6 m.

7. If the height of the house is 8 meters, about how tall is the truck?

A. 4 m.

B. 2 m.

C. 3 m.

D. 5 m.

8.

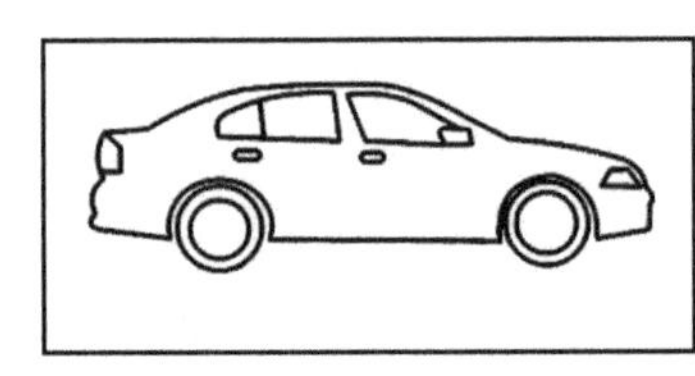

A. Grams

B. Millimeters

C. Meters

D. Kilometers

9. Which of the following is a non-standard unit of volume?

A. Kilograms

B. Cubic inches

C. Bushels

D. Hand span

10. Which of the following is true?

A. 100 cm = 10 mm

B. 2,000 m = 2 km

C. 1 km = 1,000 mm

D. 1 cm = 100 mm

Answer Key:

1) D

2) B

3) C

4) A

5) B

6) D

7) A

8) C

9) D

10) B

Lesson 4: Solving Problems Using Time and Liquid Volumes

To measure the time, we use **hours, minutes, and seconds**. For example, if the time is **6:34,** the hour is **6** and the minutes are **34**. Another way to say this is that the time is 34 minutes after 6 o'clock.

The basic units of time that we are familiar with, from the smallest unit to the greatest unit, are **seconds, minutes, hours, days, weeks, months, and years**. Second is the smallest unit of time. These units have the following relations with each:

1 minute = 60 seconds

1 hour = 60 minutes

1 day = 24 hours

1 week = 7 days

1 year = 12 months = 365 days

The U.S. customary units of capacity or volume are ounces, cups, pints, quarts, and gallons. The smallest unit of capacity is ounces (or fluid ounces). A cup is equal to 8 ounces.

1 cup = 8 fluid ounces

When we put together 2 cups, we have a pint.

1 pint = 2 cups

A quart (qt.) is equal to 4 cups or 2 pints.

1 quart = 2 pints = 4 cups

The largest unit of capacity is gallon (gal). A gallon is the same as 16 cups or 8 pints or 4 quarts.

1 gallon = 4 quarts = 8 pints = 16 cups

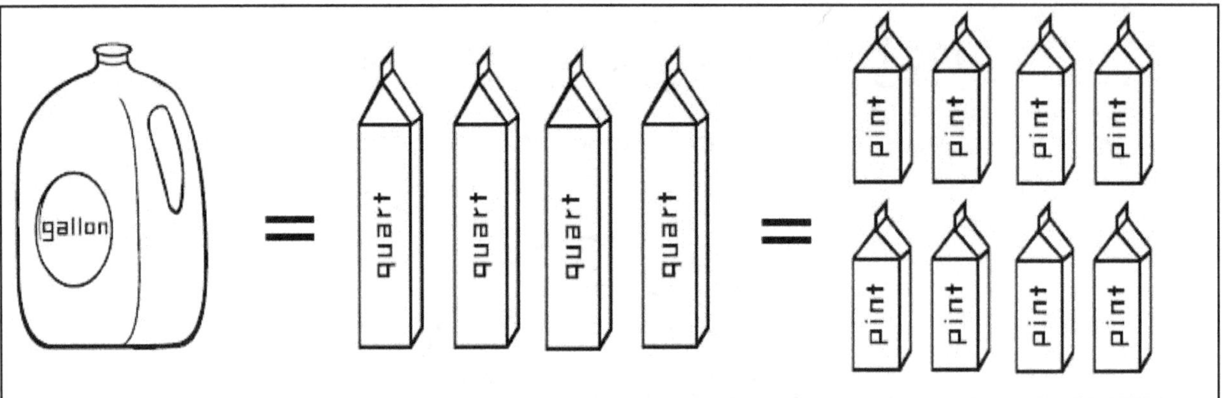

Example 1:

How many days are 120 hours?

Solution:

To convert smaller units (hours) to larger units (days), **we divide** the number of smaller units by **24.**

Recall: 1 day = 24 hours.

$$120 \text{ hours} = \frac{120}{24} \text{ days} = \textbf{5 days}$$

Example 2:

How many pints in 5 gallons?

Solution:

Identify the larger unit and the smaller unit. The larger unit is a gallon and the smaller unit is a pint.

Since we are going from a larger unit to a smaller unit, we must **multiply** to find the number of pints in 5 gallons:

$$5 \times 8 = \textbf{40 pints} \quad \text{(Recall: 1 gallon = 8 pints)}$$

Practice Exercises

1. Jeff helped his brother for 1 hour and 15 minutes. How many minutes did he help his brother?

   A. 60 minutes

   B. 85 minutes

   C. 75 minutes

   D. 80 minutes

The following table shows the time that three children studied in a week:

Name	Time
Adam	4 hours
Sophie	300 minutes
Byron	900 seconds

2. How many minutes did Adam study?

    A. 240 minutes

    B. 120 minutes

    C. 360 minutes

    D. 280 minutes

3. How many minutes did Byron study?

    A. 120 minutes

    B. 60 minutes

    C. 30 minutes

    D. 15 minutes

4. Who studied the most?

    A. Byron

    B. Adam

    C. Sophie

5. How many gallons are in 96 cups?

    A. 6 gallons

    B. 3 gallons

    C. 12 gallons

    D. 8 gallons

6. How many quarts are in ten gallons?

    A. 20 quarts

    B. 40 quarts

    C. 60 quarts

    D. 80 quarts

7. If Amanda wakes up at 6:45 a.m. and it takes her 60 minutes to get to work, at what time will Amanda get to work?

    A. 7:15 a.m.

    B. 7:40 a.m.

    C. 7:45 a.m.

    D. 7:55 a.m.

8. Clifford claims that there are x hours in one week. What is x?

    A. 144

    B. 96

    C. 48

    D. 168

9. Kathy claims that there are z ounces in one gallon. What is z?

A. 128

B. 64

C. 144

D. 136

10. An airplane departs at 1:00 p.m. and arrives at 3:15 p.m. How many minutes were the passengers on the airplane for?

A. 120 minutes

B. 135 minutes

C. 160 minutes

D. 95 minutes

Answer Key:

1) C

2) A

3) D

4) C

5) A

6) B

7) C

8) D

9) A

10) B

REFLECTION ON LEARNING

Answer the following reflection questions and feel free to discuss your responses with your teacher or a classmate.

1- What math ideas and principles did you learn in this chapter?

2- What new math concepts did you learn?

3- What procedures or methods did you practice in this chapter?

4- What aspect of this chapter is still not 100% clear for you?

5- What else do you want your teacher to know?

CHAPTER 5:
DATA ANALYSIS AND STATISTICS

Lesson 1: Interpreting Simple Data Sets, Bar Graphs, and Line Graphs

Line graphs are used to display data that changes continuously over time. They allow us to see overall trends such as an increase or decrease in data over time.

Line Graph

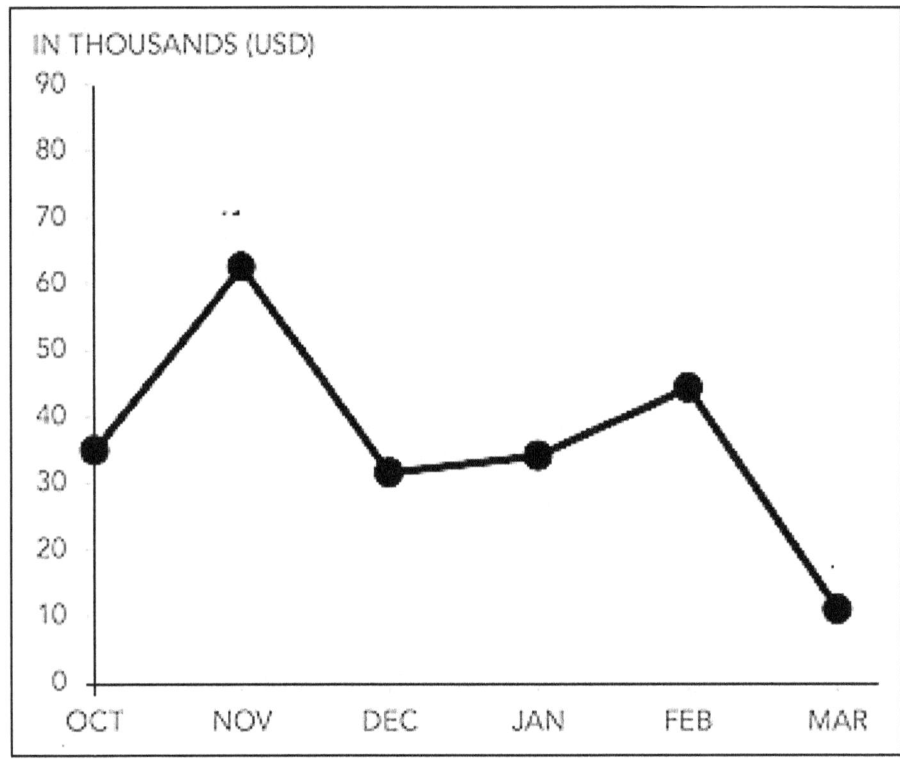

A **bar graph** is a graphical representation of data using bars or strips. They are used to compare and contrast different types of data or other measures of distinct categories of data.

Bar Graph

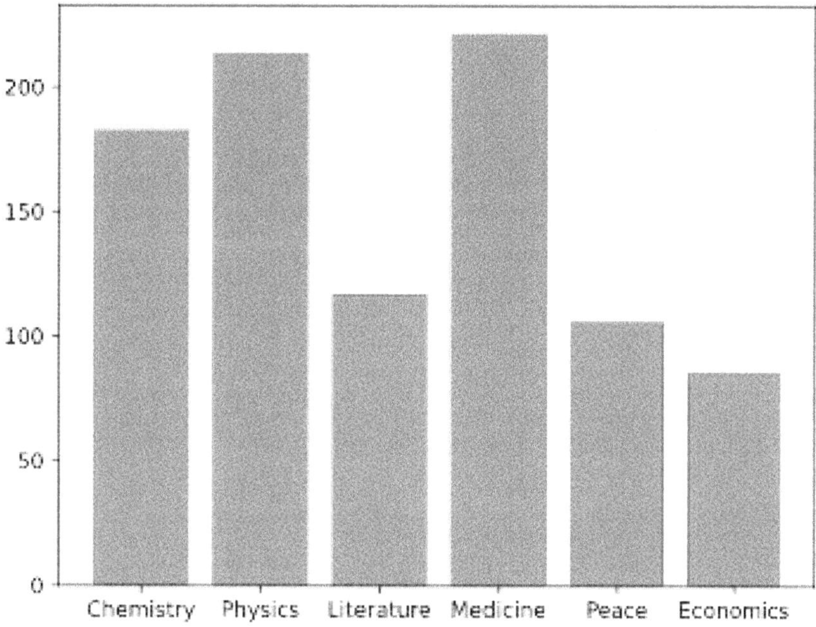

Example 1:

According to the following linear graph:

   a) Which month was the greatest price registered?

   b) What was the price of the stock share in May?

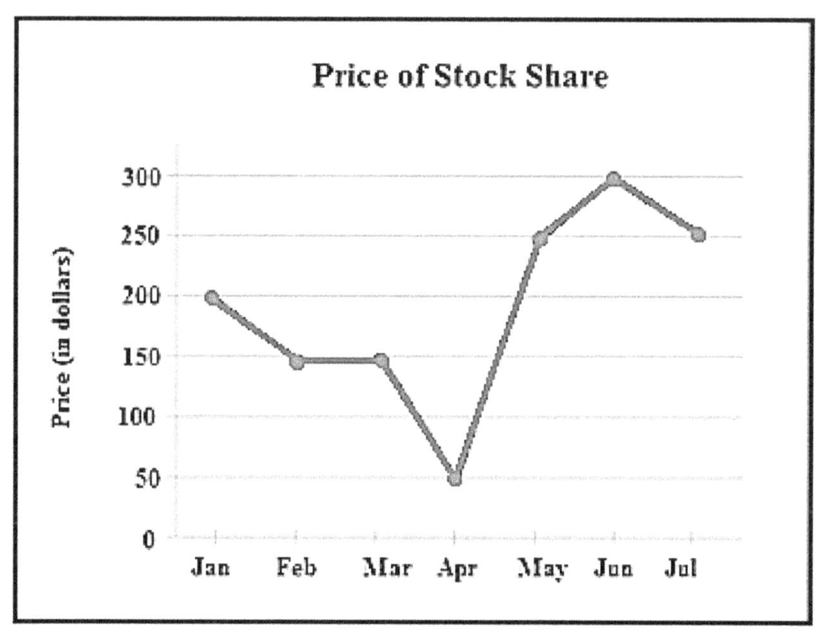

Solution:

a) Notice that the greatest price was $300. This value corresponds to **June.**

b) Notice that in May, the price was **$250.**

Practice Exercises

The following bar graph shows the number of adults who indicate the number of children they have in their families:

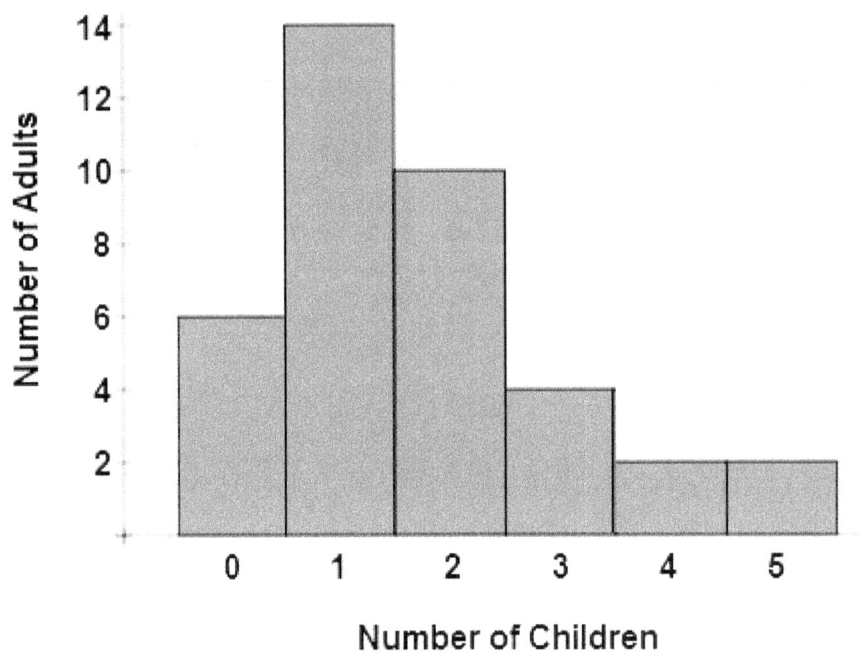

1. What is the number of adults that have three children?

   A. 5

   B. 2

   C. 4

   D. 8

2. What is the maximum number of adults questioned?

   A. 14

   B. 12

   C. 10

   D. 16

3. What is the minimum number of adults questioned?

   A. 1

   B. 2

   C. 4

   D. 3

4. What is the number of adults who do not have children?

A. 4

C. 2

B. 8

D. 6

5. How many adults were questioned?

A. 14

C. 38

B. 26

D. 36

The following line graph shows how many books were sold in a bookstore in five months:

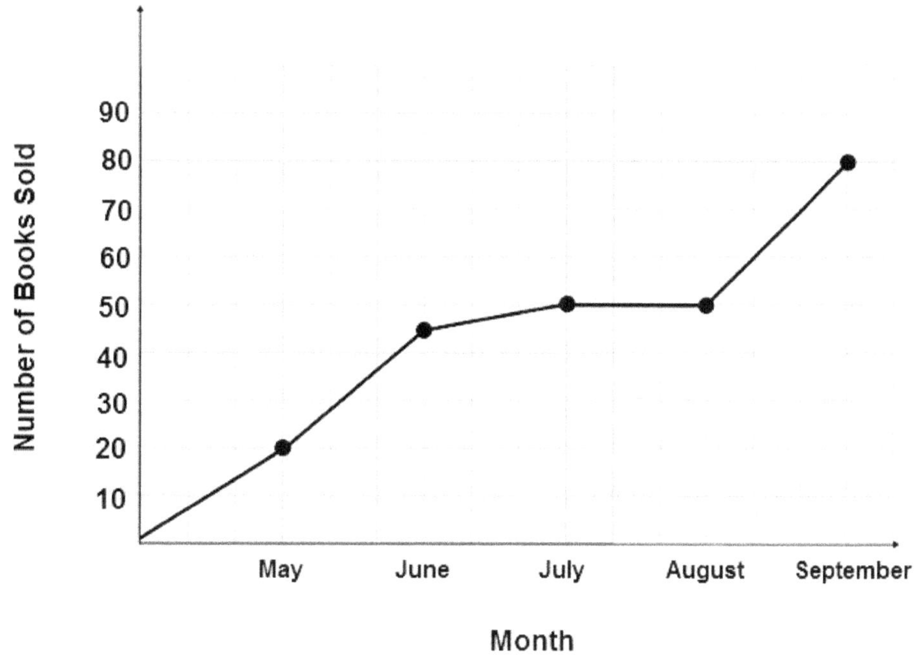

6. Which month did the bookstore sell the most books?

A. September

C. August

B. May

D. July

7. Which month did the bookstore sell the least books?

A. May

C. June

B. August

D. July

8. How many books were sold in July?

A. 60

C. 30

B. 40

D. 50

9. How many books were sold in June?

    A. 50   C. 45

    B. 40   D. 49

10. What is the total number of books sold in five months?

    A. 250   C. 240

    B. 245   D. 195

Answer Key:

1) C		6) A
2) A		7) A
3) B		8) D
4) D		9) C
5) C		10) B

Lesson 2: Solving one- and two-step problems using bar graphs

A **bar graph** is a chart that uses bars to show comparisons between categories of data. The bars can be either horizontal or vertical. A bar graph has two axes. One axis describes the types of categories being compared, and the other has numerical values that represent the values of the data.

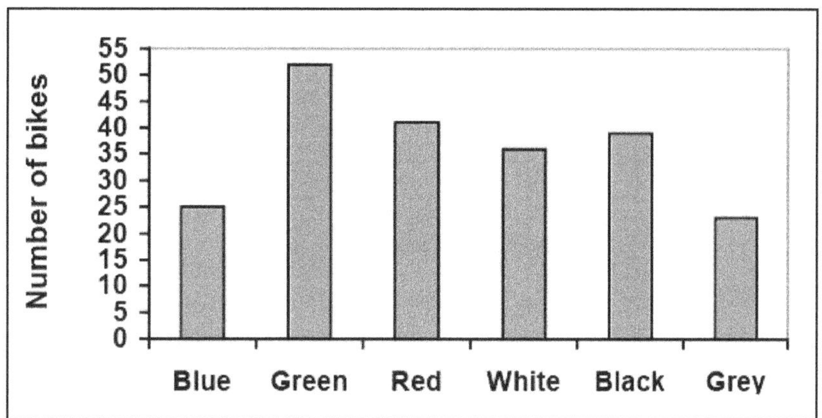

Example 1: The following bar graph shows the number of cookies made by each chef.

a)   What is the greatest value in a data set?

b)   What is the total number of cookies made?

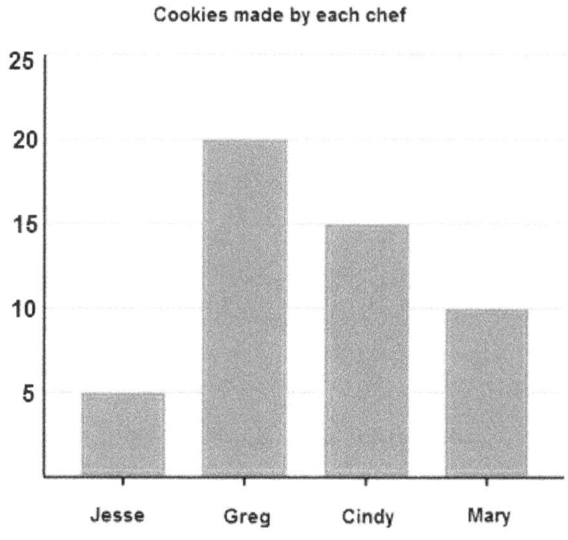

Solution:

a)   Notice that the greatest bar has a height of 20 (Greg). Then, the greatest value is **20.**

b)   To find the total number of cookies made, add the heights of the four bars:

$$\text{Total number of cookies} = 5 + 20 + 15 + 10 = \textbf{50}$$

Mr. Miller surveyed some students to find out what their favorite animals are. The results are shown in the following bar graph:

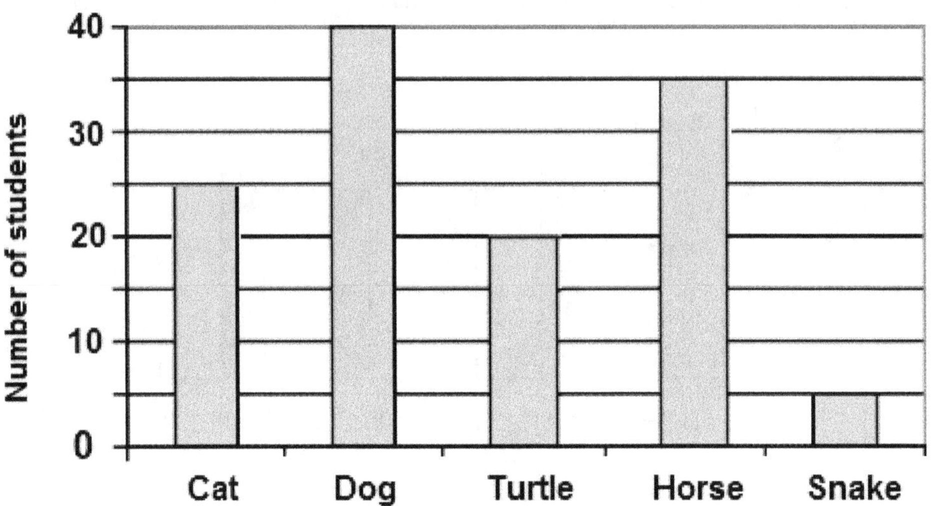

1. Which is the most popular animal?

    A. Horse

    B. Dog

    C. Cat

    D. Turtle

2. What is the least popular animal?

    A. Snake

    B. Turtle

    C. Horse

    D. Cat

3. How many students said that a horse is their favorite animal?

    A. 30

    B. 40

    C. 20

    D. 35

4. How many students said that cats or dogs were their favorite animals?

    A. 60

    B. 55

    C. 65

    D. 50

5. How many students were surveyed?

    A. 120

    B. 135

    C. 130

    D. 125

The following bar graph shows the speeds of four cars in a test drive:

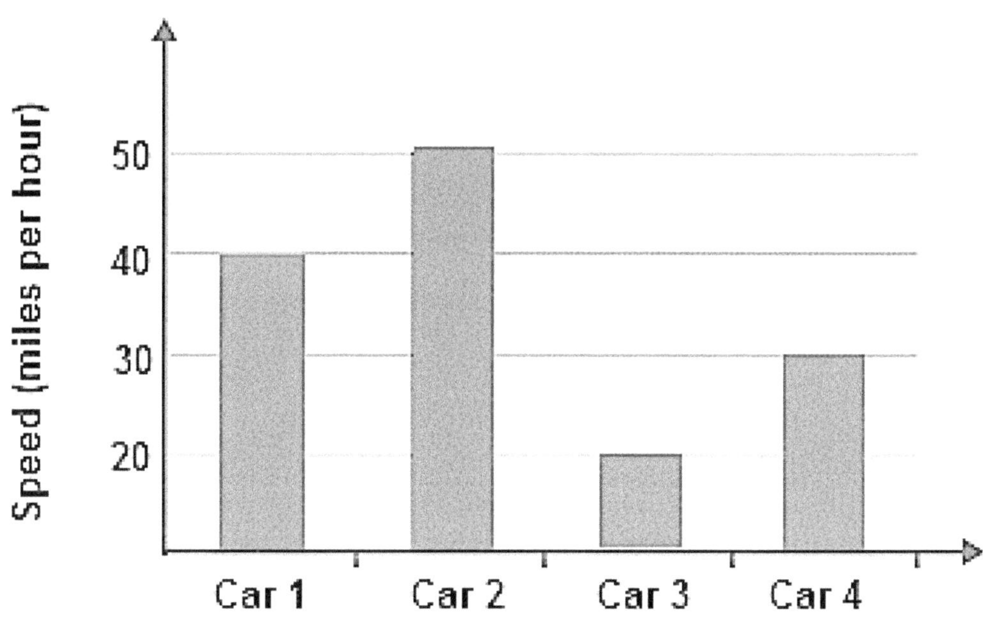

6. How fast can Car 2 travel?

    A. 30 mph.   C. 50 mph.

    B. 10 mph.   D. 40 mph.

7. How fast can Car 3 travel?

    A. 20 mph.   C. 30 mph.

    B. 40 mph.   D. 10 mph.

8. Which car is the slowest?

    A. Car 4   C. Car 1

    B. Car 3   D. Car 2

9. How much faster is Car 2 than Car 4?

    A. 30 mph.   C. 10 mph.

    B. 50 mph.   D. 20 mph.

10. A Ferrari can travel at 200 miles per hour. How much faster than Car 2 is this?

    A. 250 mph.   C. 150 mph.

    B. 140 mph.   D. 200 mph.

1)	B	6)	C
2)	A	7)	A
3)	D	8)	B
4)	C	9)	D
5)	D	10)	C

REFLECTION ON LEARNING

Answer the following reflection questions and feel free to discuss your responses with your teacher or a classmate.

1- What math ideas and principles did you learn in this chapter?

2- What new math concepts did you learn?

3- What procedures or methods did you practice in this chapter?

4- What aspect of this chapter is still not 100% clear for you?

5- What else do you want your teacher to know?

CHAPTER 6:
PURE MATHEMATICS

Practice Exercises

1. Nick saved $8,571. How do you write this number in words?

2. What is the value of A + B?

$$4,983 = 4,000 + A + 80 + B$$

3. There are 150 boxes in a warehouse. In February, 40 boxes are taken out. In March, 73 boxes are brought back. How many boxes are there now?

4. Bryan spent $84 to buy three shirts. If each shirt was the same price, what is the cost of one shirt?

5. What is the value of M?

$$15 \text{ x } 23 \text{ x } 7 = M \text{ x } 15 \text{ x } 7$$

6. Find the unknown number

$$3 \text{ x } ? = 36$$

7. Find the perimeter of the following shape:

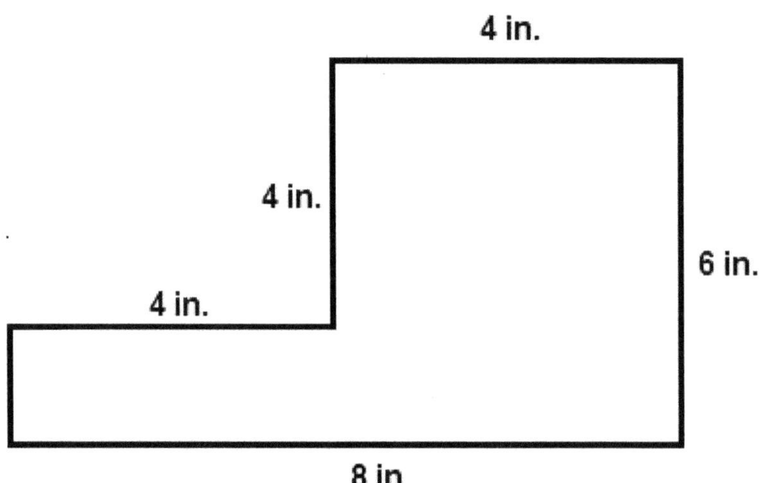

8. Laurie draws a shape that has six square faces. What shape did she draw?

9. How many minutes are there in 3 hours and 20 minutes?

10. In a jar, there are 120 ounces of water. If the jar's capacity is 1 gallon, how much more water is needed to fill the jar? (Express your answer in ounces.)

Answer Key:

1) Eight thousand five hundred seventy-one

2) 903

3) 183 boxes

4) $28

5) 23

6) 12

7) 28 in.

8) Cube

9) 200 minutes

10) 8 more ounces

REFLECTION ON LEARNING

Answer the following reflection questions and discuss your responses with your teacher or a classmate.

1- How do you feel about your performance on the practice exercises?

2- Which types of questions were difficult for you?

3- What specific things do you want to do differently next time? List them.

4- What math functions or content areas do you want to review? List them.

5- What else do you want your teacher to know?

PRACTICE TEST 1

You have 50 minutes to answer 33 questions.

1. Which is another way to show 7,090?

    A. $7,000 + 900 + 90$ C. $7,000 + 900$

    B. $7,000 + 90 + 9$ D. $7,000 + 90$

2. In the number 43,872, what digit is in the hundreds place?

    A. 4   C. 8

    B. 7   D. 3

3. A car weighs 3,575 pounds. What is the correct way to write this number?

    A. Three thousand seventy-five hundred

    B. Three thousand five hundred seventy-five

    C. Three hundred five thousand seventy-five

    D. Three thousand seven hundred seventy-five

4. A basketball team scored a total of 96 points. 53 points were scored in the first half. How many were scored in the second half?

    A. 43   C. 53

    B. 45   D. 56

5. There is a group of 20 people who are ordering pizza. If each person gets 2 slices and each pizza has 6 slices, how many pizzas should they order?

    A. 5   C. 7

    B. 4   D. 6

6. A theatre has 18 rows of seats with 9 seats in each row. How many seats are there in total?

A. 27

C. 158

B. 162

D. 33

Look at the following receipt:

```
            IKEA Food Place

               Ikea Food Fast
               89090, Food Ave
             Food City, KS, 89989
               1-888-888-8888

   Table - 05

   QTY/ Item Name          Price    Amount
   ----------------------------------------
   4   Cheese Burger        5.99     23.96
   4   Soda                 0.49      1.96
   2   Cinnamon Bun         1.00      2.00
   ----------------------------------------
   Net Subtotal                      27.92
   ----------------------------------------
   Food Tax                           2.90
   Sales Tax                          1.28
   ----------------------------------------
   Total to Pay                      32.10
   ----------------------------------------
   Received
```

7. How many items were purchased?

A. 3

C. 6

B. 10

D. 8

8. What is the subtotal amount?

A. $32.10

C. $2.90

B. $23.96

D. $27.92

9. What is the total amount?

A. $32.10

C. $3.98

B. $27.92

D. $23.96

10. Which item is the cheapest?

A. Cheese burger

C. Cinnamon bun

B. Soda

11. What is the cost of one soda?

A. $1.96

B. $1.00

C. $0.49

D. $2.00

12. What is the cost of one cinnamon bun?

A. $2.00

B. $1.00

C. $0.49

D. $1.50

13. Five friends share the cost of a restaurant bill. The bill is $60. How much does each person pay?

A. $6

B. $10

C. $12

D. $15

14. What is N?

$$4(N + 5) = 24 + 20$$

A. 12

B. 8

C. 20

D. 6

15. What is the missing number?

$$27 + 13 + 31 = 13 + \text{?} + 27$$

A. 13

B. 31

C. 27

D. 71

16. What is the unknown number?

$$50 \times \text{?} = 100$$

A. 50

B. 25

C. 2

D. 5

17. What is the circumference of a circle with a diameter of 2 feet? (Use $\pi = 3.14$)

A. 4 ft.

B. 6.28 ft.

C. 3.14 ft.

D. 1.57 ft.

18. If the radius of a circle is 1 foot, what is the area? (Use $\pi = 3.14$)

    A. 6.28 ft^2 C. 6.14 ft^2

    B. 4.14 ft^2 D. 3.14 ft^2

19. The following shape is a square. What is the perimeter of the square?

12 in.

    A. 16 in   C. 36 in.

    B. 24 in.   D. 48 in.

20. Jake drew two cylinders and three cones. How many circular faces did he draw?

    A. 2   C. 7

    B. 4   D. 6

21. What non-standard unit would we use to find the weight of a shoe?

    A. Grams   C. Fluid ounces

    B. Barrel   D. Banana

22. Which of the following is true?

    A. A meter is smaller than a centimeter.

    B. A kilometer is a metric unit of length.

    C. A spoon is a metric unit of volume.

    D. A gallon is a non-standard unit of volume.

23. How many quarts are there in 4 gallons?

    A. 1 quart   C. 16 quarts

    B. 4 quarts   D. 20 quarts

24. Brenda purchased 3 kilograms of rice, and Tony purchased 2,000 grams of rice. What is the total weight in kilograms of rice they both bought?

    A. 5,000 kg.   C. 5 kg.

    B. 2,000 kg.   D. 2 kg.

Charlie recorded how much time he studied for five months. The following line graph shows the results.

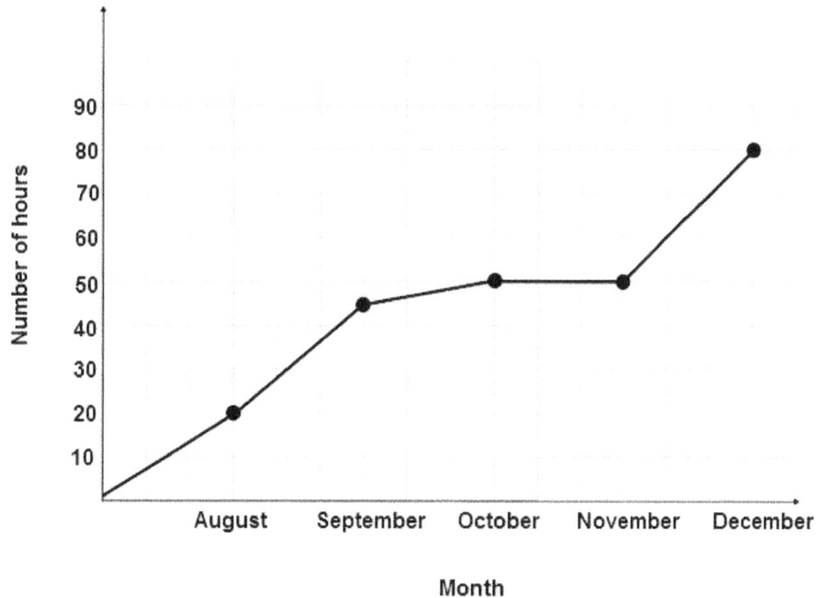

25. How many hours did he spend studying in October?

    A. 50 hours   C. 45 hours

    B. 40 hours   D. 60 hours

26. About how many hours did he spend studying in September?

    A. 49 hours   C. 50 hours

    B. 45 hours   D. 42 hours

27. Which month did he spend studying 80 hours?

    A. November   C. October

    B. August   D. December

28. Which month did he study the least hours?

    A. September   C. August

    B. December   D. October

29. What is the total number of hours he spent studying during the five months?

A. 250 hours

C. 245 hours

B. 240 hours

D. 235 hours

In a survey about customers' favorite pizza toppings, the results were recorded in the following bar graph.

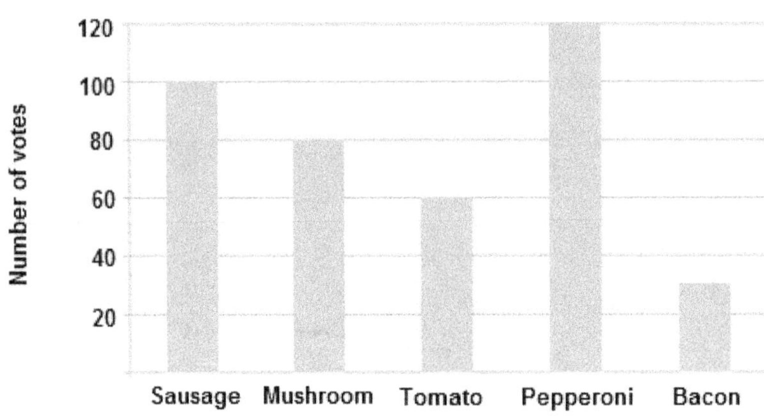

30. Which is the most popular topping?

A. Bacon

C. Sausage

B. Pepperoni

D. Tomato

31. Which is the least popular topping?

A. Mushroom

C. Bacon

B. Tomato

D. Sausage

32. Which topping has 80 votes?

A. Mushroom

C. Sausage

B. Tomato

D. Pepperoni

33. About how many votes did bacon receive?

A. 40

C. 38

B. 20

D. 30

REFLECTION ON LEARNING

Answer the following reflection questions and discuss your responses with your teacher or a classmate.

1- How do you feel about your performance on the test?

2- Which types of questions were difficult for you?

3- How do you feel about your time management strategies?

4- What specific things do you want to do differently next time? List them.

5- What math functions or content areas do you want to review? List them.

6- What else do you want your teacher to know?

1) D		17) B	
2) C		18) D	
3) B		19) D	
4) A		20) C	
5) C		21) D	
6) B		22) B	
7) B		23) C	
8) D		24) C	
9) A		25) A	
10) B		26) B	
11) C		27) D	
12) B		28) C	
13) C		29) C	
14) D		30) B	
15) B		31) C	
16) C		32) A	
		33) D	

PRACTICE TEST 2

You have 50 minutes to answer 33 questions.

1. In the number 10,647, what digit is in the thousands?

   A. 1

   B. 0

   C. 7

   D. 6

2. Jake walks 10,560 feet every day. What is this number in word form?

   A. Ten thousand five hundred sixty

   B. Ten hundred five thousand sixty

   C. Ten thousand five fifty-six

   D. One thousand five hundred sixty

3. Casey has \$56 in her checking account. How much does she have in her account after she makes a deposit of \$35?

   A. \$21

   B. \$87

   C. \$101

   D. \$91

4. Tim studied a total of 35 hours over one week. On average, how many hours did he study each day?

   A. 6 hours

   B. 5 hours

   C. 7 hours

   D. 4 hours

5. Malcom has 48 baseball cards. Greg has 25. How many more baseball cards does Malcom have?

   A. 73

   B. 32

   C. 23

   D. 33

6. What is M + N?

$$3,964 = 3,000 + 900 + M + N$$

   A. 10

   B. 54

   C. 64

   D. 15

Look at the following table:

Item	Cost
Jacket	$34
Shirt	$17
Book	$36
Coffee Maker	$60

7. What is the total cost of two shirts and a Coffee Maker?

    A. $94

    B. $86

    C. $77

    D. $84

8. If Maggie spent $68 on shirts, how many shirts did she buy?

    A. 5

    B. 4

    C. 3

    D. 6

9. Which item is the cheapest?

    A. Jacket

    B. Coffee Maker

    C. Shirt

    D. Book

10. If Mr. Wallace has $200, what is the maximum number of jackets he can buy?

    A. 5

    B. 8

    C. 3

    D. 6

11. Sarah claims that there are N dimes in $10. What is N?

    A. 10

    B. 50

    C. 100

    D. 25

12. What is M?

$$8 \text{ quarters} + 10 \text{ dimes} + 20 \text{ nickels} = M \text{ dollars}$$

    A. 5

    B. 3

    C. 2

    D. 4

13. What is the value of P?

$$5 \times P \times 31 = 23 \times 31 \times 5$$

A. 23   C. 31

B. 5   D. 36

14. Which expression is equivalent to 20 x 18?

A. 5 x 4 x 1 x 8   C. 18 (10 + 2)

B. 20 (5 + 13)   D. (6 x 3) + 20

15. What is the unknown number?

$$? + 25 = 85$$

A. 110   C. 50

B. 65   D. 60

16. When 12 is subtracted from a number, the result is 16. What is the number?

A. 4   C. 28

B. 30   D. 24

The following figure is a rectangle:

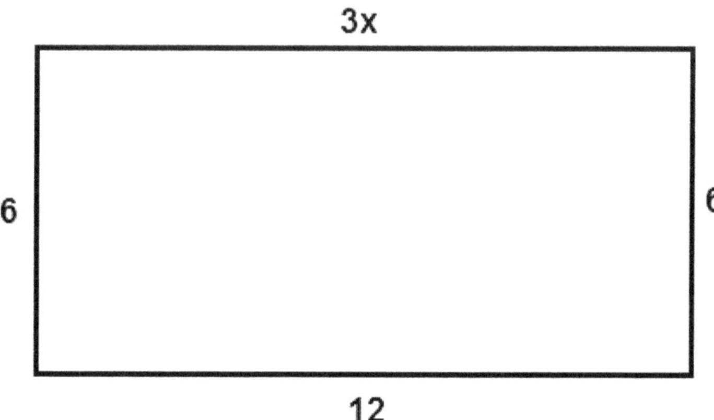

17. What is x?

A. 6   C. 12

B. 4   D. 8

18. What is the perimeter of the rectangle?

    A. 36   C. 24

    B. 18   D. 32

19. What is the area of the rectangle?

    A. 72   C. 18

    B. 36   D. 12

20. If the perimeter of a square is 8 feet, what is the area of the square?

    A. 2 ft^2.   C. 6 ft^2.

    B. 4 ft^2.   D. 8 ft^2.

21. Which unit is most appropriate for describing the weight of a dog?

    A. Grams   C. Gallons

    B. Kilometers   D. Kilograms

22. Which of the following is true?

    A. Kilogram is a non- standard unit of capacity.

    B. A sandbag is a non-standard unit of weight.

    C. Fluid ounce is a metric unit of weight.

    D. Two quarts is greater than one gallon.

23. How many days are there in six weeks?

    A. 42 days   C. 35 days

    B. 21 days   D. 14 days

24. Adrienne practiced her dance routine for 35 minutes. She stopped practicing at 5:15 p.m. What time did she start practicing?

    A. 4:45 p.m.   C. 5:50 p.m.

    B. 4:40 p.m.   D. 4:50 p.m.

25. Pete arrived at the museum at 1:30 p.m. He left at 2:36 p.m. How many minutes was Pete at the museum?

    A. 36 minutes   C. 64 minutes

    B. 52 minutes   D. 66 minutes

26. Henry has a fish tank with a capacity of 2 gallons. He uses a 2-cup bowl to fill the tank. How many bowls of water does he use?

A. 32

B. 16

C. 42

D. 12

27. A water tank had 80 gallons of water in it. After it rained overnight, there were 85 gallons of water in it. How many quarts were added to the tank?

A. 5

B. 15

C. 10

D. 20

The number of absentees in a math class was recorded in five months. The following bar graph shows the results.

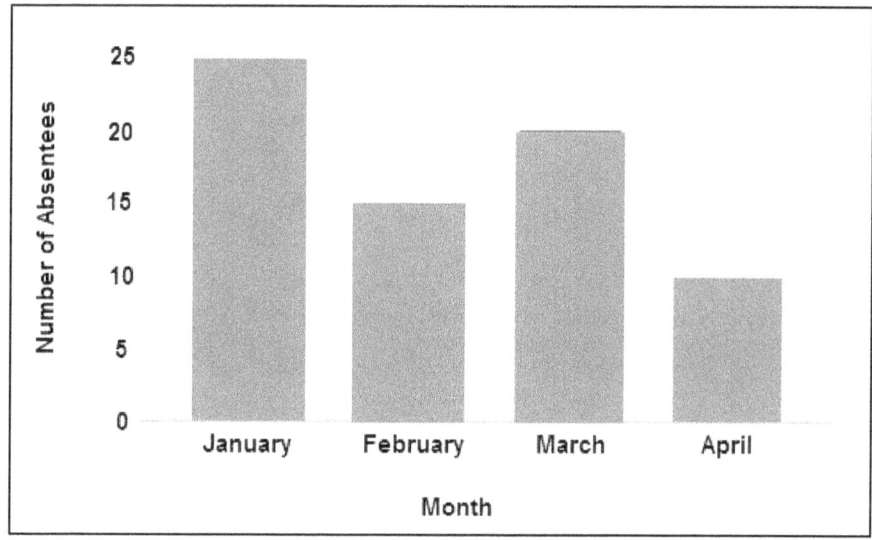

28. In which month was the maximum number of students absent?

A. March

B. February

C. January

D. April

29. In which month was the minimum number of students absent?

A. January

B. April

C. March

D. February

30. How many students were absent in February and March?

A. 15

B. 35

C. 20

D. 25

31. What is the total number of absentees in the five months?

   A. 65

   B. 60

   C. 55

   D. 70

32. Emily drew three triangles and five pentagons. How many sides did Emily draw?

   A. 34

   B. 25

   C. 28

   D. 36

33. What is the missing side length of a triangle whose perimeter is 72 inches and the two sides are 18 inches and 24 inches?

   A. 26 in.

   B. 30 in.

   C. 32 in.

   D. 25 in.

1)	B	18)	A
2)	A	19)	A
3)	D	20)	B
4)	B	21)	D
5)	C	22)	B
6)	C	23)	A
7)	A	24)	B
8)	B	25)	D
9)	C	26)	B
10)	A	27)	D
11)	C	28)	C
12)	D	29)	B
13)	A	30)	B
14)	B	31)	D
15)	D	32)	A
16)	C	33)	B
17)	B		

REFLECTION ON LEARNING

Answer the following reflection questions and discuss your responses with your teacher or a classmate.

1- How do you feel about your performance on the test?

2- Which types of questions were difficult for you?

3- How do you feel about your time management strategies?

4- What specific things do you want to do differently next time? List them.

5- What math functions or content areas do you want to review? List them.

6- What else do you want your teacher to know?

MORE TEXTBOOKS BY CBL

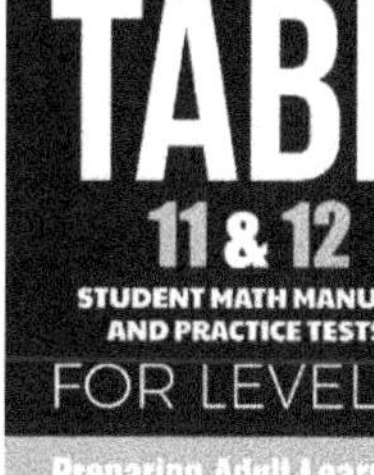

ADULT ED
MATH
NUMBER SYSTEM, NUMBER SENSE, AND OPERATIONS PREPARING
FOR
CASAS, TABE 11 & 12, HISET, AND GED TESTING
BY COACHING FOR BETTER LEARNING

ADULT ED
MATH
GEOMETRY PREPARING
FOR
CASAS, TABE 11 & 12, HISET, AND GED TESTING
BY COACHING FOR BETTER LEARNING

CBL COACHING
FOR BETTER LEARNING
Math
Practice Worksheets and Workbook for Adult Students
A learner-centered tool designed to help students practice and master the four operations while preparing them for CASAS Math GOALS 2, TABE 11 and 12, ACT, HISET, GED tests, and IET programs.

SKILLS FOR SUCCESS IN CAREER AND TECHNICAL EDUCATION (CTE)
STUDENT GUIDE
A SYSTEMATIC WAY TO MASTER ORGANIZATIONAL AND SOFT SKILLS
CBL COACHING
FOR BETTER LEARNING
BY COACHING FOR BETTER LEARNING, LLC

HOW TO ACHIEVE BETTER STUDENT RETENTION IN ADULT EDUCATION
Secrets to becoming an indispensable adult-ed teacher that provides a learning experience that's hard to walk away from (and keeps administrators happy!)
TEDDY EDOUARD

TABE 11 & 12
CONSUMABLE STUDENT READING MANUAL
FOR LEVEL E
Preparing Adult Learners for TABE 11 & 12 Reading Tests and for Vocational Training and College Entrance Reading Exams
By Coaching for Better Learning, LLC

TABE 11 & 12
CONSUMABLE STUDENT READING MANUAL
FOR LEVEL M
Preparing Adult Learners for TABE 11 & 12 Reading Tests and for Vocational Training and College Entrance Reading Exams
By Coaching for Better Learning, LLC

TABE 11 & 12
CONSUMABLE STUDENT READING MANUAL
FOR LEVEL D
Preparing Adult Learners for TABE 11 & 12 Reading Tests and for Vocational Training and College Entrance Reading Exams
By Coaching for Better Learning, LLC

TABE 11 & 12
STUDENT LANGUAGE MANUAL
FOR LEVEL E
Preparing Adult Learners for TABE 11 & 12 Language Tests and for Vocational Training and College Entrance Exams
By Coaching for Better Learning, LLC

TABE 11 & 12
STUDENT LANGUAGE MANUAL
FOR LEVEL M
Preparing Adult Learners for TABE 11 & 12 Language Tests and for Vocational Training and College Entrance Exams
By Coaching for Better Learning, LLC

Preparing Adult Learners for TABE 11 & 12 Math Tests and for Vocational Training Entrance Math Exams
TABE 11 & 12
Consumable Student Math Workbook
FOR LEVEL E
By Coaching for Better Learning, LLC

Preparing Adult Learners for TABE 11 & 12 Math Tests and for Vocational Training Entrance Math Exams
TABE 11 & 12
Consumable Student Math Workbook
FOR LEVEL M
By Coaching for Better Learning, LLC

Preparing Adult Learners for TABE 11 & 12 Math Tests and for Vocational Training Entrance Math Exams
TABE 11 & 12
Consumable Student Math Workbook
FOR LEVEL D
By Coaching for Better Learning, LLC

Preparing Adult Learners for TABE 11 & 12 Math Tests and for Vocational Training Entrance Math Exams
TABE 11 & 12
Consumable Student Math Workbook
FOR LEVEL A
By Coaching for Better Learning, LLC

CBL COACHING
FOR BETTER LEARNING
Workbook
Number and Letter Tracing for Adult Students
This tool is designed to help adult students practice and master handwriting. It is appropriate for literacy, ESL, and ABE classes.

READING NOTEBOOK & JOURNAL
For Adult Students
By Coaching For Better Learning   CBL COACHING

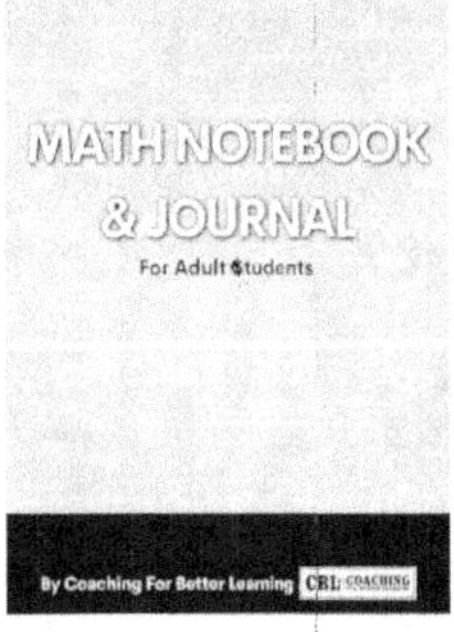

MATH NOTEBOOK & JOURNAL
For Adult Students
By Coaching For Better Learning   CBL COACHING

BOOK 1
PHONICS AND LIFE SKILLS READING
FOR
Adult Literacy, ABE, and ESL Students
Turning Learners into Proficient Readers
CBL COACHING
FOR BETTER LEARNING

BOOK 2
PHONICS AND LIFE SKILLS READING
FOR
Adult Literacy, ABE, and ESL Students
Turning Learners into Proficient Readers
CBL COACHING
FOR BETTER LEARNING

BOOK 3
PHONICS AND LIFE SKILLS READING
FOR
Adult Literacy, ABE, and ESL Students
Turning Learners into Proficient Readers
CBL COACHING
FOR BETTER LEARNING

About CBL

At CBL, we promote systematic solutions, learner-centered textbooks, and forward-thinking strategies in adult education, workforce development, and vocational training. Our diverse solutions and products are intricately designed to enrich students' learning experiences while making the job of busy, hard-working adult instructors easier.

CBL takes pride in publishing student-centered textbooks designed to prepare learners for CASAS, TABE 11&12, HiSET, and GED assessments and assist instructors in covering course curricula and standards with confidence.

Our publications also include teaching guides, test prep tools, and study guides that foster reflective learning, ensuring sustained engagement in active learning. Find our meticulously crafted textbooks on our book page (cbledu.com) or major platforms like Amazon, Barnes & Noble, and Ingram Spark.

CBL also guides adult education and workforce programs in establishing robust professional development programs—training, peer-mentoring, coaching, community of practices (CoPs), and instructional systems— fostering a culture of continuous improvement and contributing to higher learner retention and success rates. We also offer workshops and PD sessions for adult educators and classroom instructors.

If you have suggestions or questions about instructional systems, textbooks, or student learning and retention, contact us today at teamcbl@cbledu.com or 410-960-4082.